Empathy and Eyebrows

A SURVIVALIST'S STORIES ON REVIVING YOUR SPIRIT AFTER SOUL-CRUSHING SH*TSTORMS

Danni Starr

WISE Ink
CREATIVE ★ PUBLISHING

ISBN: 978-1-63489-092-2
EISBN: 978-1-63489-093-9
Library of Congress Catalog Number: 2017952043

Printed in the United States of America
First Printing: 2017
21   20   19   18   17   5   4   3   2   1

Cover Design by Emily Mahon

Wise Ink Creative Publishing
837 Glenwood Ave.
Minneapolis, MN 55405
www.wiseinkpub.com

To the three most important people in my life:
My daughters and my best friend Claire.
May you always see yourselves and love yourselves
the way that I do . . .

and to Beyoncé, Thank you for spending three days with
me in a closet and for getting me back in
formation. #iaintsorry

Thank you, God. Thank you, Universe.
Thank you, ancestors.

Foreword

I MET DANNI when she was Danielle. She was a freshman and I was a junior, so I had no reason to know her, but I did. Because if Danni is around, you have no option *but* to know her. She has the same light and energy now that she did at age fourteen. She emits the undeniable sense that she is Someone and she is Going Somewhere.

This book is not about that. Or it is, but it isn't. It's about what happens when a woman loses her sense of self to work, to family, to bad relationships both personal and professional.

Most of us have been there at some point. I know I have, at least, though Danni and I arrived at that hopeless place in different ways.

That isn't the important part, though. We all fall. We all struggle. We all have days . . . weeks . . . months? . . . when nothing is right and everything feels too hard and even our eyelashes hurt. (That can't just be me, right?)

The important part is what we do with that struggle. Not just the crying in public part (my personal favorite), but the lessons you take from it.

This is about feminism and amateur stripping, being a good parent and leaving a bad marriage. It's about racism and sexism and what it takes to get yourself back from everyone who chipped away at you, little by little.

It's better when Danni tells it, trust me.

xo,
Nora McInerny,
Speaker and author of *It's Okay to Laugh*
(Crying Is Cool Too)

London

> "The most common way people give up their power
> is by thinking they don't have any."
> —Alice Walker

I'M SITTING IN a café in London. They are blasting American music, but I just had an English breakfast and am drinking tea out of an oversized cup. This is happening. I did it. This is *Eat Pray Love* and I am Julia Roberts. I'm Bulia—black Julia! I got here on a Virgin America flight (and FYI, if you gotta fly somewhere, seriously, go Virgin America. It was like a damn party. Food, entertainment, and the bathrooms were *huge*). So, yes, I got here by plane, but how did I really get here? Why am I really sitting in a London café? The truth is, I lost myself.

Ruin is the road to transformation. I believe this. I wholeheartedly, with every breath that I take, believe this. I'm sure that ruin looks different for everyone. For me, ruin is a constant place of self-doubt and questioning. I wanted so badly to believe that things were okay and that I had found my happily-ever-after that I smiled through pain, laughed when I wanted to cry, and agreed to things I really didn't want.

Love is a beautiful thing, but it can be deceiving. Love made me love someone else so much that I forgot to love myself first. It may seem impossible to forget how to love yourself, but I've done it. I've lived it, and it's tragic. When I no longer recognized myself, it was time to do some soul-searching. I traveled to the Caribbean alone with a baby. I went to a week of intense therapy. I spoke to the people I love the most and asked, "Have you seen her—the woman I used to be? She went somewhere, and I don't know how to get her back."

I prayed. For me, for him, for the girls. I prayed all the time. *Help me be the best partner, the best mom.* I prayed for balance. I prayed like I always do: *Dear God, help me be the best me that I can be.* A shift happened. A spark in my spirit, if you will. I saw glimpses of her, and I began to remember her. I missed her.

She was gone for a long time, trapped in depression, anxiety, and a marriage that gave her two beautiful girls and a friend for life in their dad but also damaged her soul.

I spoke to her like an old friend. *Hey, I know things have been really tough, and no one knows the real struggle but us, but I really like when you're around. So I was thinking that you shouldn't go ghost on me again. The last couple of years without you, I almost didn't survive. I'm gonna need you to ride or die with me.*

I'm gonna need you to remember who you are. Before you were ever anyone's wife or mom, you were a powerhouse ready to change the world. Don't ever forget that.

Things are going to look and feel different from here on out. She is back! She is me and finally I am she and damn it feels good. Here's to finding, knowing, and loving ourselves always.

The Blood of Christ Be with You

I GREW UP with an abusive, alcoholic father. I know that sounds terrible. My dad was a dick, but fortunately he had some redeeming qualities. He told the best jokes, cooked amazing breakfasts, and made up bedtime songs that lasted so long that all us kids stayed up way past our bedtime. My dad was awesome, until he wasn't. Alcohol is my dad's nemesis. I'm not sure when it grabbed ahold of him and decided never to let go. My dad was drunk the day I was born and pretty much every day after. For the most part, it's the only way I ever knew him.

It's not an exaggeration. My mom has told me plenty of times that my dad and my uncle Gil showed up to the hospital and passed out the day I was born. The only thing my dad remembers about that day is that I pooped on him. He used to tell me the story, and when he got to that part, he would pause, look me in the face and go, "And then you shit on me!" I would laugh and think to myself, *Yeah, well, you've been shitting on me ever since, so I guess we're even.*

On my first communion, we high-fived after I drank the blood of Jesus. I gave him a thumbs-up and a huge smile. "It was good, Dad!" I said, and he laughed that big belly laugh that I inherited. Now, as an adult, thinking about that kind of breaks my heart. Most kids bond with their dads over sports or just spending time together. At the tender age of nine, I knew that the best way to bond with my dad was to throw back wine like a pro and like it. The blood of Christ be with you.

Alcohol got the best of my dad on many occasions. When I was a child, he went to rehab a few times. One time, it was a live-in facility, and he was there for months. I imagine it wasn't voluntary and that he probably got a DWI or something that forced him to go. Even so, he did the entire program, and we were there to watch him graduate. I was really excited. *Could this be it?* I thought. *Dad's done drinking, whoo whoo!* Family members of the other people in treatment got up and spoke about their loved ones. Even though we didn't know each other, we shared a common bond of understanding what it feels like, how bad it hurts, to love an alcoholic.

My mom spoke. I can't remember exactly what she said, but she sounded hopeful and she looked proud. I bet all hope was lost when we went to Applebee's after Dad's ceremony. My dad can't be the only one to graduate from treatment and celebrate with a beer, right?

One day my dad came home from work and he was belting out this ridiculous song: "Oooooh, going out the door. I'm a loser, baby, so why don't you kill me." I asked him what he was singing, and he went on and on about how he wrote the song that day at work. I believed him. It was a stupid-ass song. He totally could have written it. Years later, I was in the backseat of a minivan heading to my varsity middle school basketball game and a familiar tune came on the radio. I start singing along and then yelled, "Hey! This guy stole my dad's song!" When the words escaped my lips, I realized how insane that sounded. That guy, by the way, was Beck, and he did not steal my dad's song. Quite the contrary.

Because my dad is an amazing liar, he is also an amazing storyteller. He sucks you in, and you literally believe every word. He has been caught in the middle of Compton Crips and Bloods, found a bag of money after a botched robbery, written a rap song called "Hard-Core Dope," been shot in the butt by his best friend Cory, and partied with some of Cali's finest, including Ice Cube. Some of these stories are true. I've done the research, and they've checked out. Others I'm not too sure about.

I've imagined my dad's death. I have intrusive thoughts, and he stars in them often. The thing is, my dad dying isn't really all that unbelievable. He really did spend most of his life, and all of mine, drinking himself into an early grave. Even as a recovering alcoholic, he's done an unspeakable amount of damage to his kidneys and liver, and he now suffers from pancreatitis.

I will be given the task of writing his eulogy. I will stand at the podium dressed in black and I will tell stories. I will talk about his big game at Minneapolis South High School, the one where he had more yards than anyone on any other team, and he did it without catching a pass. It was all kick returns and punt returns. I swear I heard Al Bundy from *Married with Children* tell a similar story, but whatevs.

I will tell happy stories of floating down Apple River, camping, and his sobriety and what it meant to his children. I will avoid at all cost the bad stuff. It's his funeral, his highlight reel. Punching your wife in the face, throwing beer in her eyes, wrestling with her in front of your young kids—that's not stuff people want to hear at a funeral.

Nobody wants to hear that I became an expert at silently dialing 911, that I stood in the corner for over a day because I refused to admit to doing something I really didn't do, that my little brother's sternum still cracks when he breathes in because dad punched him so hard when we were kids.

I will force out of my head the sound of my mom's screams, the look of pure terror on my little brothers' faces, and the anger on my older brother's face because he couldn't protect his mom. I try really hard to find the good in even the worst of situations, and the only good thing that I can think of to come out of dad's alcohol addiction is the fact that he can't remember much of the abuse he caused. And that's only good for him.

I'll tell happy story after happy story, and everyone will laugh. They will shake their heads in agreement, and he will be celebrated. He passed down his amazing storytelling talent to me. I will stand up there and do him proud, and it will all be the truth, every last word of it—well, most of it. I will be retelling stories he told me, and we all know he mastered the art of fabrication.

I didn't speak to my dad for a long time. I couldn't understand how he could choose alcohol over his family. When dad got sick and almost died, the doctor told him it would kill him if he continued drinking. He drank anyway. When they tell you doing something will kill you and you do it anyway, that's not a choice; that's addiction. I learned to love my dad despite his being an addict. I'm so glad I finally learned to separate the addiction from the person. It wasn't easy, but it was healing. After years of holding on to anger over my relationship with my dad and his relationship with alcohol, I let it go. I forgave, I loved, and I rebuilt something that I thought was beyond broken. It wasn't and I'm thankful.

My dad stopped drinking a few years ago on January 29, which just so happens to be my birthday. He's been pretty much sober for a few years. I say "pretty much" because he has slipped up a few times and wound up back in the hospital.

I realized I had only known my dad drunk when he came to visit me sober. I watched him play with my daughter. He told the same outrageous stories but in a different way. He asked me if I was doing okay. He emotionally connected with me. I was used to Drunk Dad, so Sober Dad was overwhelming. I told him I needed to go downstairs to check the mail. Instead, I sat in the game room of my apartment complex and cried. I had just spent five days meeting my dad for the first time, and it was beautiful.

Déjà Vu

TIANA IS THE daughter of my mom's older sister Julie. Auntie Julie lives in California, so Tiana and I don't get to see each other that often. The problem is that, when we do see each other, shenanigans ensue because we are kindred spirits in every way possible, including the worst ones.

I was home from college one summer, and Tiana randomly called me. She told me they were coming to visit and that I needed to find her a strip club so she could do amateur night. She said nobody knew her in Minnesota and she needed to make money. Made sense to me, so I went to work. Minneapolis has an array of strip clubs—in my later years I would frequent them often—but I was barely over eighteen and I knew nothing about the strip club scene. I welcome a challenge, though, and so by the time Tiana arrived with all her stripper ambition I knew just the place—Déjà Vu!

I still remember how nervous I was watching her clumsily swing around the pole. If I was nervous just watching her, I couldn't imagine how nervous she must have been up on the pole, but she did it. For the entire week she visited, we spent every night at the strip club, her on the pole and me acclimating myself to stripper life without actually being a stripper. I became a stripper den mom, if you will. When the ladies needed something, I was the person who got it. I figured it would be more comfortable for me to run and grab something, seeing as how I didn't have a G-string riding up my ass.

Tiana owned her week as a stripper. She was on a damn mission, and I was along for the ride. By night four, she looked like a real-deal pro. (Okay, she was mediocre at best, but still I stood there behind sniffer's row, beaming with pride.)

I was terrified her mom would find out and kill us. I wasn't really worried about my mom; she retired from stripping when she found out she was pregnant with me, so she really had no ground to stand on.

It was the strip club that taught me that I spend too much time overanalyzing things. While everyone around me was enjoying the show and making it rain, I was wondering how the hell they keep the pole germ-free. I thought about the acrobatics of everything and pondered how many times the strippers had fallen trying to perfect a move. I questioned what went on in the backroom. Seriously, what happens in there? I people-watched like crazy, giving every person a story. The guy Tiana was giving a private dance to was cute. I named him Alex and decided he was a father of two, unhappily married, and a high school principal. I wondered what would happen if one of his former students hit the stage. What would he do? Would he hide? Throw money? I had clearly been in the strip club for entirely too long. I was giving backstories to creepy-ass men.

There is no one type of exotic dancer. Trust me—I was den mom for a week, and I learned a lot. Some strippers are on their quick grind like Tiana. Others really are stripping their way through school. Some are moms. Some strip part time, while others are seasoned professionals and it's strip or die for them. I'm not really one to knock anyone's hustle, but during my week as den mom at the 'Vu, I saw a visibly pregnant stripper, and I draw the line there. Take your pregnant ass home.

Tiana made her money and headed back to Cali. I kept her secret.

Years later, equipped with the knowledge to secure a win at amateur night, I returned to Déjà Vu dressed as Jane from Tarzan. My mother—who, as previously stated, had knowledge in this arena—helped me pick out my costume. I enlisted the help of a few friends who I was comfortable enough with to let them see me butt-ass naked. During my week in the strip club as den mom, I learned that it really doesn't matter how good you are at working the pole. When it comes to amateur night, you just have to have the loudest crowd! I could handle that, and for a few minutes of nakedness I would walk away with five hundred bucks!

I was backstage, holding my whip—because, look, if I'm gonna be a stripper, you better damn believe I'm using props and I'm going all out—and I could hear my friends cheering. I was a little nervous and a little excited. The club manager tapped me on the shoulder. Okay! This was it. It was go time.

"Sorry, hun," he said. "You were the only person who showed up for amateur night tonight, so we gotta cancel it." Divine intervention at its best.

Repeat After Me

I ONCE HAD a coworker call me when I was home alone with the girls. I was instantly annoyed when he asked me if I could put my kids away. No, I'm sorry, I'm not gonna kennel my kids. Besides, it's just me and the girls, so if you want to talk to me, you gotta deal with the occasional outburst from one of my offspring. He was frustrated that I asked why he wasn't in a meeting. I was not sure why he would be frustrated by this. It was a logical question. If we were having a team meeting and a team member was missing, it made sense that someone would ask why the whole team isn't present.

He told me that we were not equal, that he went above our managers to upper management and got the okay to miss the meeting. I was irritated already. Did he just say we were not equal? I didn't need a lesson on equality. I'm multiracial and a woman, so I know a thing or two about not being equal. He told me that people need to be checked sometimes and that this was him checking me. Yes, you read that right. I am a grown woman, a mother, and someone's wife. Did this fool just tell me he was checking me? Oh hell no! I was not gonna let this man—who was not my husband, father, brother, or any man of real importance in my life—talk to me this way, especially because my husband, father (Sober Dad, at least), and brothers would never talk to me this way. Just as I fixed my lips to respond, he continued, "You're a mother and the breadwinner of your family. If I were you, I wouldn't do anything to jeopardize that." Yup, he went there. This motherfucker just threatened me.

"Did you just threaten me?" I asked. "Because I really don't do well with threats."

He told me that he was trying to help me, to "protect" me and my family. He continued on about checking me. Mind you, this entire time I was praying to God to keep my mouth shut. Tears were streaming down my face, not because I was sad but because I was mad as hell and I literally couldn't cuss his ass out because he held all the power in this situation. "This is the conversation that Tony Fly never had with you. This is the conversation that Sam Elliot (a former boss) never had with you. This is me checking you."

Oooooh, so now you are a mind reader, a psychic? You just know the conversations I had with former coworkers and friends? My mind was racing, my heart pounding. I had to get off the phone. He had been going on for an hour now. It was the most ridiculous conversation I had ever had, and it got worse.

Sensing that I was clearly upset, he knew it was now time for the pick-me-up. Abusers do this. They will beat the hell out of their spouses and then show up with flowers, jewelry, or a card. Hey honey, I'm sorry I nearly choked the life out of you, but these sunflowers, man, I just knew you had to have them! Fuck you and your sunflowers. So there he came with his peace offering. "You know you're my secret weapon. I need you to believe that." Dude! You just belittled the hell out of me for an hour. Are you insane? I seriously needed to get off the phone. I was shaking and sweating, and it was past the girls' bedtime.

Him: Repeat after me. "I'm a boss." You're a boss. You know that, right?

Me: I'm not doing that.

Him: "I'm a boss." Say it.

Me: I. Am. Not. Doing. That.

Him: Do it or I'm not getting of the phone.

Me, defeated: I'm a boss. Okay, I really gotta go.

Him: Okay, before you go, I need you to give me one good takeaway from this conversation.

I couldn't make this shit up if I tried.

Me, rolling my eyes and through tears: You care about me a lot. I gotta go.

What the fuck was that? I was sitting in the kitchen, emotional as hell, on a chair built for a toddler. I couldn't work with people like this. I didn't care what the hell I had to do. I'd rather be broke and happy than secure and miserable. I couldn't do this. I was thinking purely emotionally. I needed someone to give it to me straight. I called Tony Fly.

Get Back on the Pole!
(Tony Fly)

I'VE SPENT SOME of the best nights of my life with Tony Fly. Quality human being, this guy is. I grew up listening to Tony Fly on the radio, so yes, I almost dropped a deuce in my pants when he wanted me to be his cohost. My first day on the job, I was so starstruck that I literally didn't speak. That's kind of a problem when you're a radio personality. After the show, my boss asked me how my first day was. I told him amazing and that it was so crazy that I was working with *the* Tony Fly. He said, "That's great, Danni. But if you don't talk, I'll fire you." I gave up being a fan and instead became Tony's life partner. I was twenty-one, working with this amazing radio family. I was living the dream.

One night, after a fight with Best Friend Claire (BFC) the whole show was out at a nightclub. I don't smoke, I've never smoked, but I was drunk, I was fighting with my best friend—and, well, YOLO. Tony went outside for a smoke break. I drunkenly followed behind him, took the cigarette out of his mouth, and start to smoke. He was laughing, but after just one hit, I vomited on his shoes. Now, most people probably would have called it a night, but the night was young and so was I and we had a strip club to visit!

Everybody walked into the 'Vu—yes, that 'Vu, my old stomping grounds—but not me. I literally looked like I was on skates. I could barely stand, but I said, "I got this!" Strippers love women clients. I sat in the front row, and the next thing I knew, I was half naked. A hush came over the crowd. "Is that Danni's titty?!" "Danni's titty!" "Awwww shit, Danni's titty." I don't think I really need to tell you this, but my titty was out. The stripper was fast, man. I didn't even see it coming! Our show crew was cheering and making it rain, but not Tony. "Somebody get Danni and put her titty away!" he said.

I woke up the next morning in my studio apartment with no pants on. Oh shit! Oh shit, is somebody here? OMG, Danielle, what did you do? Why do I not have any clothes on? I was looking for signs. I picked up my phone to call Tony and his wife, Kiona. One unread message alert:

D, You passed out. We brought you in the house, now get up, lock your door and call me.

I spent five years as Tony Fly's cohost. Most men I've come across have tried to dull my shine. They've been intimidated by my strong opinions and the fact that I hold my own. When I became well-liked or more successful, they treated me differently and even tried to get rid of me, but not Tony. Tony told me I was gonna be a star, and he really believed that. He never stood in the way of anything. Tony became my family. I have loved him for over a decade. He gets me.

After that conversation with my coworker, I was in need of somebody who got me. I reiterated the conversation to Tony. He was pissed, but Tony always remains logical. He told me that I deserved to be where I was and that I worked my ass off to get there so I shouldn't let someone try to run me out. He knows me, though. He knew that I don't operate like that. I need to be around good people or my spirit suffers. "I can't do this, T!" I said, and when I said it, I really believed it. But then Tony gave me an analogy that changed my world.

"You know how there are strippers that are just strippers? Then there are strippers who really are stripping their way through law school. You are a stripper! Every day you get your ass back on that pole because you are stripping your way through law school. Law school for you is getting hired by the TLC network, magazine covers, documentaries. Just stay on the pole."

The next day as I headed into work, I texted Tony:

Me: *I'm ready for today. I got this. Just a stripper getting through law school.*
Tony: *It's like survivor . . . outwit outlast.*

I don't know what it was about that analogy, but it worked. I powered through the ridiculousness that I was surrounded by. It really was like a season of *Survivor*, and I was on Crazy Island. Tony would check in daily with his favorite stripper. I told my closest friends about the analogy, and I would get texts throughout the day reminding me to get back on the pole or to work it.

My entire mentality shifted. If my coworkers said something to me, I would politely respond, but in my head I was watching a stripper work the hell out of the pole.

I got back on that damn pole daily. It became my routine. I was doing so good too. I was killing it at work. Getting on the pole became second nature, so the craziness literally wasn't bothering me. But then, one day, I fell off the pole.

Universal Intervention

SOMETIMES YOU JUST can't deny the power of the universe. A while ago I watched, and then posted, some of Jane Elliott's work—her Blue Eye–Brown Eye study and a lecture she gave. I was in awe of this firecracker of a woman. There is something so beautiful about people who do social justice work. It's not easy work. It wears on your spirit, and many times while you are searching and trying to create good you get a lot of bad thrown back at you. I fell in love with Jane instantly. I had been conflicted lately. I didn't know what I wanted to do. I had been looking into social work, criminal justice, getting my master's in journalism. Hell, what was one more giant transition in a long list of never-ending transitions? I had felt stuck, but an unexpected encounter at an Airbnb changed my life.

I needed to find a place to stay in Iowa. Of course, of all the potential options, I picked the Airbnb owned by Jane's daughter. Hello, universal intervention. So I sat for hours and spoke with this now-eighty-three-year-old impassioned firecracker of a woman, and I damn near cried. She told me of her good friend Killer Mike and how rapper T.I. used her voice in one of his songs. We talked about justice and change, and I entirely leaned in to the conversation. I talked to her about raising two little girls and the challenges I have faced as a very vocal and passionate woman . . . and woman of color at that. She spoke, I listened, I learned, and I felt the universe working in all the right ways.

She gave me a list of books to read and even read some quotes out loud to me. One of those quotes was about breathing in atoms and breathing out atoms and how being in contact with others is how change happens—because regardless of whether we try or not, we are constantly giving away pieces of ourselves and taking pieces of others. I quickly chimed in, "So you need to surround yourself with only good and positive people."

She looked at me and, to summarize, told me, "No, surround yourself with people who are not like you, because they need our positive energy. The exchange of energy happens regardless, so why only surround yourself with like-minded people? How will that bring about change?"

I must have hugged her twenty-five times. I was trying to breathe in all of her freedom-fighter magic. I think the universe was trying to tell me something. I could have been anywhere—I could have picked any number of places to stay—but instead I landed on the doorstep of a woman who, just recently, was put on BBC's 2016 list of the most influential women in the world. A woman who has spent her life fighting for social justice. So no, I don't have all the answers, but I know one thing: I do not believe in coincidences.

I'm a Feeler

WHEN I WAS about eleven years old, I learned one of my greatest lessons—intuition is not something to be ignored. One evening, my mom asked me to walk with her to the store. She was a single mom at the time and couldn't drive because she was legally blind, so walking was often our form of transportation.

When we arrived at the store, we saw a very odd man. The moment I locked eyes on him, the hair on my arms stood straight up. That had never happened to me before. I instantly knew that something was wrong. I couldn't explain it, but everything inside of me told me that something was not right. Years later I would discover a word for this—empath.

I told my mom that the man made me uncomfortable. She initially shrugged it off. As we strolled down the aisles, the man was always just a few feet away from us, always within eyesight. I reiterated my discomfort to my mom, and this time she paid closer attention. I told her that I was not leaving the store with this guy around. As we were approaching the checkout lane, my mom told me to walk toward the door and yell back to her that dad was waiting outside for us. In reality my dad wasn't even around at the time, but my mom thought it was a good idea for the man to believe that we had a man waiting for us to exit the store. After that announcement, the odd man left. I watched him get into his truck and drive off. It was the first time since entering the store that my breathing normalized. We finished ringing up our items and got ready to head home.

As we left the store, we took a shortcut home that had us walk down an alley. I have no idea why that seemed like a good idea, but it was cold outside and Minnesota winters can be horrendous, so I'm assuming we just wanted to hurry up and get home. The alley that we were walking down split in the center and became a T. A person coming down the alley could either continue straight or turn midway through to go down the T. As we walked, my mom and I were randomly talking. I remember looking at her and saying, " All I know is if I see a truck, I'm out." As soon as I said the words, bright headlights appeared, and a truck came right at us. Fight or flight kicked in with a mixture of panic, and my mom ran up the T and I ran down it. I found an industrial-size garbage can and went behind it. It was up on four wheels, though, and I kept thinking, *Oh God, if he looks under, he will see me.*

I did the only thing I could think of. I put my feet up on the garbage can and I put my hands on the fence behind me. I hoisted myself and I held my breath. At this point, the odd man had gotten out of the truck. I could hear him crunching in the snow and getting closer. I glanced over my shoulder and wondered if I could quickly flip over the fence and run back to the store for help. I decided that I probably wouldn't have enough time to make it over before he grabbed me. I knew he was close. I could still hear crunching and breathing on the other side of the garbage can. I had never been so scared in my life.

The crunching grew quieter, and I could tell he was retreating. I was shaking profusely, holding on to the fence and the garbage can, and I was terrified he was going to hear me. I heard the sounds of his door opening and closing and his truck slowly pulling off. I waited for what seemed like forever until it was silent. I hopped down from the garbage can and screamed for my mom. I heard her yell back, and as I ran toward her voice, the odd man flipped his lights on and hit the gas out of the driveway. He had pulled in and shut his lights off to hide. He flung his door open and grabbed me. I screamed and thrashed, trying to get out of his grasp. He was driving and dragging me, and I knew how this ended: I died. If he got me in his truck, I would die. The next thing I knew, I was being pulled by a superhuman force from the other side. My blind-ass momma came to my rescue from out of nowhere and pulled us both to safety. She than proceeded to move faster than my legs could carry me. To be clear, she dragged the hell out of me. We exited the alley to the actual street and we approached a house. Back then, McGruff Houses were plentiful, so I assumed that's where we were heading. My mom threw open the porch door of a random house and literally Chuck-Norris-karate-kicked the main door in. She screamed at the top of her lungs, "Help us! Call the police."

As we sat there, waiting for the police with the people we had just scared the life out of, I glanced at my mom and realized she was still holding the groceries. My mind was blown. How the hell did she manage that? I sat, watching her and trying to calm my heart rate.

Finally I was able to speak. I said, "Mom, you still have the groceries." Without even missing a beat, she replied, "Yeah, because I still have hungry babies at home."

Brother David

WHILE I WAS putting the final touches on this book, my high school teacher Brother David passed away. It shook my world. Brother David was vital to my spiritual awakening. He taught a class called Comparative Religion. People talked about Brother David like he was impossible. They warned me to not take his class. The workload he required was intense, and he wasn't exactly charismatic, but there was something extremely lovable about him.

Brother David's class dissected the five major world religions. He was a Christian Brother, yet he taught the class very objectively. I learned so much and, to this day, I still retain what I learned from his class. Brother David didn't just teach me about religion and spirituality. He also taught me a very important life lesson.

In order to get an A in his class, it wasn't enough to be above 90 percent. It was also required to turn in a five-page paper comparing different aspects of the world religions. Now, the paper was optional, but if you chose not to turn it in, you wouldn't get your A. I had a 98 percent in Brother's David class, but back then a five-page paper seemed like the end of the world. My GPA was a 4.0, so I figured taking the B wouldn't hurt me too much.

The due date of the paper came, and as Brother David walked around the room collecting the papers of those who decided to turn it in, I ducked my head and pretended to be invisible. He stopped at my desk and waited. I didn't know if he thought a paper was going to magically appear, but it wasn't. He told me that he wanted to see me after class and continued on his way.

I was terrified. The paper was optional, and I took the option of not doing it, so why did he want to see me? As my classmates trickled out of the room, I sat there. This man sat behind his desk and stared me down. I didn't know what to do, so I just stared back. Finally, he spoke. "I expect to have your paper turned in on Monday." Was he referring to this optional paper, or did he just give me a special assignment? "You deserve your A, so I look forward to reading your paper on Monday," he continued. I attempted to bring up the optional part of the assignment, but he just stared at me like he didn't understand my words. So I spent the weekend writing a five-page paper comparing the lives of Buddha and Jesus, and thanks to being forced to write the paper, I did get my A in Brother David's class. I only spent a trimester with him, but he taught me so much.

I learned tolerance and acceptance. I learned that, for the most part, the core values of the world religions are similar and that I am much more of a spiritual person than a religious person. I learned a lot about expectations. People will rise to expectations, but they will also fall to expectations. My expectations of myself were much lower than Brother David's expectations of me. This man forced me to do an optional paper, and I am so thankful that he did. Sometimes people will think higher of you than you think of yourself. Sometimes they will push you because they see something in you that even you don't see; let them. And sometimes they will have zero idea the impact that they had on your life.

During the summer of 2016, I ventured back to my old high

school stomping grounds. I pulled up to a building that was much more modern than the one that I remembered. So much had changed, but as I headed inside, I crossed paths with someone very familiar. I think I probably startled Brother David with my excitement. I ran up to him as if he were in the hottest band and I were a groupie. I was beaming. "Brother David, you might not remember me, but Comparative Religion changed my life. Easily my favorite class of all time. Brother David, can I hug you?" I was concerned that I might have gone too far because Brother David didn't like to be touched, but this was the only moment I had with him and I needed to shoot my shot.

Brother David really didn't get a word in, but he looked amused. "What's your name?"

"Danielle, class of 2003, and I love you, Brother David." I leaned in for the hug.

When I caught back up with Ms. Hanson, my once senior year English teacher but now forever friend, I was over the moon! "I. Hugged. Brother. David. . . . And he asked my name!"

Thank you for believing in me, Brother David. Thank you for seeing more in me than I saw in myself. Also, thank you for the hug. I am fully aware that was way out of your comfort zone. Rest in peace, good sir. You've changed lives.

What I Really Meant to Say Was

OVER TIME, I developed this really terrible habit of not saying what I really feel. My guess is that my constant need to feel accepted and liked played a major role. When I was incessantly worried about a person's response or feelings, it was much easier to tell them what they wanted to hear instead of telling them the truth or telling them my feelings.

I watched beautiful friendships turn toxic. I watched relationships sour. Like a plant I watered daily, I felt resentment grow inside of me. The thing is, by telling half-truths, by agreeing when I didn't want to, by always saying yes, by placing everyone else's feelings above my own, I was watering resentment, and it was suffocating.

I spoke to my dad for years even though every time I did my feelings were immensely hurt. He was capable of making me cry with just the tone of his voice, but he was my dad and I felt like I had to speak to him. So I would answer the phone and listen to his drunken babble and always end the conversation with an, "I love you, Dad. Talk to you soon."

What I really meant to say was: Dad, I love you, but you make me sad. You make me angry. I hate everything about the way I feel when I talk to you. So, until you get it together, don't call me.

A really handsome guy with an amazing voice and I were randomly going on dates and spending time together. When he asked me to be exclusive, everything in my mind screamed no. I wasn't ready. I wanted Rumspringa! Rumspringa, by the way, is when the Amish kids go out and get buck wild for a year or two and then decide if they want to go back to the culture they know and love or give it up for good. I wanted that! I mean, me and Handsome Sexy Voice Guy, we had a good thing. He made me laugh, I felt wanted, and the sex . . . well, there was a lot of that, and it was good. But exclusive? God no. Of course, I told him yes.

What I really meant to say was: I'm not ready. No, I am not ready! This is great the way it is, and I like you. But Rumspringa is calling my name. Can I have both?

A coworker told me that I had only gotten this far in my career because I was a hot girl who had everything handed to me. I sat silently and cried the ugly cry. Seriously, Kim Kardashian's ugly cry had nothing on this.

What I really meant to say was: You know what, I did look pretty cute when I became the first person in my family to graduate from college—oh, and magna cum laude—and I was probably cute when I was the keynote speaker for the American Heart Association's national conference—so cute that they made me a national spokesperson. I must have been cute as hell to work for free for two years at a radio station because I wanted the opportunity so bad. You know what's really cute, though? When you date your boss but refuse to let him give you a raise because you never want anyone to accuse you of sleeping your way to the top. Don't get me wrong, I have definitely smiled my way out of a speeding ticket or two, but I am where I am because I am, and have always been, a motherfucking grinder. Don't you ever let these dimples fool you.

Time and time again, people would tell me how amazing me and my husband were together. They would tell me about my beautiful family. They were so happy that I was happy. They would ask me how we did it, and I would smile and say, "It's hard work, but really good work."

What I really meant to say was: Look, this is the hardest shit I have ever done. I came into this marriage as a powerhouse, and now I don't even know who I am. I'm not happy, he's not happy, but we take amazing photos. I don't know how to get out. I'm stuck. I love him and my girls, but this, this isn't it. Help me.

Never Send a Dick Pic

ONE DAY, a coworker came to work and was instantly frustrated because the Wi-Fi wasn't working. Though I understood his frustration—it is difficult to do a radio show without Wi-Fi—the way he went about trying to get it fixed was all wrong. He was extremely rude to our IT guys. He called one of our higher-ups over speakerphone and yelled about the Wi-Fi. It was mad uncomfortable. It was a full-on temper tantrum—grandstanding, if you will. I texted my supervisor and told him I was uncomfortable and that the situation was anxiety-inducing. My boss told me he would handle it. At some point, my coworker got in another member of the show's face. He was yelling and telling him he would replace him, and I'd had enough. This tantrum lasted entirely too long. I was silent, and then he looked over and said, "Does anybody else have anything to say?" I told him that I was uncomfortable, that he had been yelling for the past two hours, and it was making me anxious. I said it in a calm voice. He then leaned over the board and told me that I needed to calm down.

My mind was blown. He had spent the last two hours screaming about Wi-Fi, yelling in people's faces, and screaming at management, and he had the audacity to tell me to calm down. He literally told me that I was scaring the interns. This is what they call gaslighting. He told me that I was aggressive and angry. What I was not about to do was sit there and be Angry Black Woman-ed. I remember exactly what I said. I told him that he had never seen me angry; in fact, how I was right then and how I am when I'm actually angry are vastly different, but I would gladly show him if he needed to see the difference. He told me I needed to take five. At this point, I was angry. I had experienced too much of his BS. There were times when he would say live on the air that I was looking at him crazy or giving him crazy eyes. I wouldn't even be looking at him. I said on the air multiple times, "Please do not make me out to be an Angry Black Woman, because I am not." I stood up and I told him that how he talked to people wasn't okay. I told him that other people might be okay with the way he talked to them but I for damn sure wasn't going for it. I got ready to leave, but not before telling him to get his shit together. It wasn't hard to understand; I simply didn't want to be talked to a certain way. I figured that management would control their talent, that we would have a sit-down and work it out. What I could have never anticipated was how the next few weeks would play out.

I was kept off the air, all the while being reassured that I was going to return. During the hiatus, I decided that, since I had time, I would start the notes for the book I had always wanted to write. Somehow, my book notes, which had absolutely nothing to do with any radio drama, made somebody uncomfortable. I got a call from a coworker who told me that everyone wanted me fired and that he was trying to save my job. Apparently I was making it difficult since I was writing a "tell-all" book about him. I laughed. What the hell did I look like writing a book about him? I knew it wasn't true anyway. We'd had other conversations where he threatened me or tried to scare me into submission. Nobody wanted me fired. (Well, maybe one other person, but that person didn't matter because they didn't play a role in hiring or firing, and honestly, they just didn't want to like me due to their own insecurities.) It just didn't make sense. I was killing it on air, the sales people loved me, and I had never, even been reprimanded for anything. More than that, though, there were no grounds to fire me. So that's exactly what I said. To my surprise, he replied, "Well, I wouldn't be so sure about that because somebody saved a certain dick pic." I was like, WTF. I knew exactly what he was talking about because I actually had sent him a dick picture.

Months prior to all of this, we were doing a bit about inappropriate text messages. We were talking about how everyone has that one asshole friend who knows when you are in an important meeting and sends you an inappropriate text. My coworker was saying how it never failed to happen when he was sitting on a plane next to an old lady. We were all laughing. It was all within the context of the show. BFC was listening and thought it would be hilarious to join in on the fun, so she sent me a dick pic. Let me be clear that this was a dick that neither of us knew. This was a damn stock-photo dick pic that I was being threatened over. I was laughing so hard, and my coworker asked what was so funny, so I forwarded him the text. Again, this was all on the air, in context, and he laughed. I had no idea that it would ever be used against me.

The thing is, I am sure this behavior is frowned upon in most professions, but not in radio. I was a lady in a locker room. The things I heard and witnessed were often disgusting and over the top. For the most part, it didn't bother me because some of it came with the territory. I also wasn't a stranger to inappropriate jokes. I grew up with five boys. So imagine my shock when my coworker uttered those words, "Well, I wouldn't be so sure about that because somebody saved a certain dick pic." So what! First, it was a part of a bit, and second, the amount of disgusting talk heard daily both on and off the air is proof enough that he wouldn't be offended by a dick pic. Nevertheless, he made the threat, and I got off the phone shocked.

The next morning I groggily woke up and answered my phone. My coworker told me that this was my olive branch, that the listeners were getting riled up, and that I needed to go on the air and help calm them down. By this point, I had been off the air for a while and nobody was talking about it, so listeners, rightfully so, were wondering where I was. Meanwhile, I didn't go any-damn-where. I was at home twiddling my damn thumbs. So we went on the air, and I just remember I kept saying that I couldn't wait to be back. It felt like a setup. Something wasn't right, so I just wanted to make it very clear to the listeners that I wanted to come back, so I said it repeatedly. Afterward, he thanked me and I went back to sleep, thinking, *Well, hopefully this can finally blow over.*

My feeling of being set up was right, though, because after I was used to calm down the listeners, he followed through on his dick pic threat. It was completely premeditated. He knew the listeners were concerned. They knew something wasn't right, and he wanted to make sure the listeners heard us sounding chummy so that when I never came back it wouldn't fall back on him. It was genius, pure evil genius.

When HR called me, I thought for sure they were calling on my behalf, until they asked me about the dick picture. I told them that I knew exactly what they were referring to, since he had threatened me with it the night before. I explained the entire story. I told them that if they had ever listened to the show, they would know how ridiculous this was. I then made it clear that I wasn't going down without a fight. The audacity of someone to accuse me, a mother of two, of being a sexual offender. The audacity of a man who had told me the most vulgar of sexual escapades on multiple occasions to feign being appalled by a stock-photo dick picture. I quickly told HR that if we were going to use jokes as reality I had some of my own to add to that game. I let them know that every time my coworkers came over they would bring a watermelon and chicken and that that was "very offensive." I didn't actually care about that because, stereotypes aside, I like chicken and watermelon. The point was, hell no, they were not going to use a joke as reality and think I was just gonna sit back and take it. I told the HR rep I had multiple scenarios and I could do it all day. She told me that wasn't necessary. Of course it wasn't! How could a man who told me that he once "fucked a girl who put ping-pong balls in her pussy" and how it reminded him "of Mike Wazowski from *Monsters Inc.*" really be offended by a stock-photo dick picture? I made my point, got off the phone, and spent days in bed. I couldn't believe the manipulation.

About twenty-one days later—because, you know, it took that long to clear me of being a sex offender—I found myself sitting in an office with upper management. They looked upset. I was told I was cleared of any wrongdoing which, of course, I already knew. They then told me that they needed to make some programming changes and that I would not be returning to the show. I sobbed, straight ugly-cried. I didn't even want to work with someone like that, but I couldn't believe we were really sitting here avoiding the fact that a psycho set me up with a dick picture and pretending it was about programming changes. I pulled myself together and asked them not to insult my intelligence. I was smart enough to know this had zero to do with programming changes. This was all about money. Because the host of the show was a huge asset to the company, it was easier to dispose of people around him, which happened often, than to get rid of him. He was a cash cow, and he knew it, so he made his own rules. And they cleaned up his messes. I'm not sure how I found the words, but they came. "What we are not gonna do is sit here and pretend this is about programming changes. How about we don't do that."

I never got to say good-bye. I just disappeared like I never even existed. I heard lies told about me and what I was doing, and I was muzzled. I had put my heart and soul into my job. I loved it, and I loved the listeners, and I just disappeared. I've got to hand it to the evil genius, though. I'm sure he knew I wouldn't be reprimanded for sending him the picture—it was a bogus claim—but once you accuse someone of sexual misconduct, personnel isn't going to let you work together again. That's some serious, well-thought-out fuckery.

I wanted to fight. I wanted to tell everybody. I always fight against injustice, so I had to fight for myself, right? I was tired, though, straight emotionally exhausted, and I wasn't sure I had it in me. I met with a lawyer who told me I had one hell of a case, and still I wasn't sure I had the energy to fight. I opted out of staying with a company that would allow what happened, and I also opted out of fighting. I was raising two little girls, and I needed to make sure they were okay no matter what, and the best way to do that was to try to get as far away from the situation as possible. The entire thing was messing with my mental health. I would lie awake at night wondering how the hell it could all have happened. I was the provider of my family; how could a person literally try to destroy my life? Coming for me was one thing, but this would have an impact on my babies. I was pissed.

I want to be very clear: I firmly believe all of this happened because I was good at my job. That sounds crazy, right? I was good at my job, and it made other people uncomfortable. Listeners would call in and say hi to the show and then yell that they loved me, and my coworker would remind them of the name of the show, as if everybody didn't know. In meetings with higher-ups, they would point out that I was a secret weapon and that I brought something different to the show. I remember one time being pulled aside and having a highly respected talent coach tell me that I was killin' it. He told me that he used me as an example of a strong female lead in his morning show boot camps. I was proud of myself but also happy that he did not say this in front of anybody else. I didn't want to be in competition with my teammates. When I won, we all won. And when they won, I was winning too.

It happened, though. As we all gathered around, the talent coach announced to the entire group what he had said to me, and things changed the very next day. The entire dynamic of the show was off. Can you imagine how bad it feels to feel bad about being good at something? What if Serena Williams felt bad every time she walked out on the court because her talent made other people uncomfortable? That's how I began to feel. I should have been celebrating my growth within the industry. I should have been proud of my accomplishments. Instead, I felt like there was now a target on my back. Considering I was later set up with a dick picture, I guess there kind of was.

I cried a lot during this time. I thought about all the BS I had put up with. The racial side-comments. The time I was asked to stop doing so much charity because it was making the rest of them look bad. The racist-ass phone call where a white man who claimed to have "jungle fever" said that a black woman could teach him things that his white girlfriend couldn't—like how to "gorilla fuck." His girlfriend, by the way, kept making sarcastic comments about the black woman and what she could possibly teach him. "Like what, how to enunciate?" That phone call didn't air, but it probably would have had I not been in the room. I say this because, except for the only other minority in the room, all the males found this hilarious. I then spent hours explaining to my boss why this was offensive—not just the call but also the re- action of my coworkers. I really didn't feel like giving him a life lesson on racial sensitivity, but he continued to ask questions. I finally told him that if he didn't get it after my third time trying to explain it, then I couldn't help him and he needed to do some soul-searching because it wasn't my job to explain to anybody why blatant racism is upsetting. I will never forget what he said to me: "Well, in their defense, they're white so maybe they just don't get it." I was done. I know a whole heap of white folks who would have been equally as offended as I was.

It wasn't even just a black-and-white issue. Had the call been sexist, homophobic, etc., I would have had the same response. The call was wrong, period. My coworker called me later that day and asked why I wouldn't just tell him I was upset. I had never been so mad at the world. Let me break it down. I was upset because I shouldn't have to tell a grown-up that racism has an impact on me, saddens me. I was upset because it didn't affect or sadden him. I was mad that I spent hours trying to help people understand why we couldn't be a show that ever allowed something like that to happen.

That was literally the worst day of my radio career. My

then-husband and I weren't even really on speaking terms at the time, but I called him because I needed someone to hear me. He never really heard me, so I am not sure why I chose to call him. He must have heard the defeat in my voice, the pain, because for the first time in a long time I heard it in his voice too as he whispered, "I am so sorry, Danielle."

I got home from work that day and went straight to bed. I slept so hard that I overslept the next day. I woke up to a ton of missed phone calls and texts. I hurried and called the producer of the show. I told him I was on my way, that I overslept, and that I was sorry. He told me to hurry because the host was "super pissed."

So he's mad about tardiness but not racism? Oh, I see, only things that affect him. I went off. "Fuck him, I said I'm coming! If I didn't have to spend hours yesterday talking to people about racism, I probably wouldn't have cried myself to sleep and over-slept due to emotional exhaustion." The producer apologized and said he didn't know and told me he would notify the rest of the show that I was en route. By the time I got to work I had whoo sahhhh-ed enough to be completely normal. I walked in and told my coworker that I was sorry and that it wouldn't happen again.

He looked at me, raised his hands, and yelled, "Where ya been?"

He knew where the hell I had been. So I looked back at him and said, very matter-of-factly, "I said I was sorry. It won't happen again, but I don't need a lecture." Of course he told me I was being aggressive. I wasn't.

We clearly needed to have a meeting. I said that we all needed to have a coming-to-Jesus meeting and turned my upper body and used my hands to emphasize all of us. I was then accused of lunging at a coworker. I wound up sitting in a meeting with him, and he said he feared for his life. I laughed. Every man on the show was easily double and or triple my size. They had thrown things at each other out of anger, one time even a futon, and yet none of them had ever said they feared each other or for their lives. I'm a black woman and this happens all the time. I'm not "allowed" to be passionate; instead, I'm called angry. I am not "allowed" to be strong in my opinions because then I'm a bitch. I was clear in the meeting. I told them that this was happening because I was a woman. I left out the black part because I already knew what it was, and sometimes having to explain that part to people who don't care or don't understand . . . well, it's not my damn job. I also was raised with five boys who taught me how to defend myself, so if I would have lunged at my coworker, I wouldn't have stopped mid-lunge. I believe in follow-through.

What happened to me was awful, absolutely awful, and at the time I was devastated. I realize now, though, that I probably would have stuck it out. I had to provide for my babies no matter what. So even though the situation was no longer serving me, I would have done my job well even if it hurt to walk in there every day.

The universe is beautiful. Knowing I wouldn't walk away, the choice was made for me. Surely I don't believe the universe wanted me to be set up with a dick picture, but I do believe that what happened to me happened *for* me. I've also learned that after something really horrible happens in my life, something really amazing usually follows it—checks and balances—and it keeps me humble. I also believe in karma, just sayin'. One more thing: never send a dick pic.

Reality TV

EVERYONE ALWAYS ASKS me about my time in reality TV: if I regret it, if it was real, what really happened. The truth is, I only ever really wanted to do *The Real World*, and I came close to doing it. I was the first alternate for the DC season, which is kind of crazy since I would later end up living in DC. *Bridezillas* started off as a joke. I had never even seen the show. One night, the kids I was nannying were channel surfing when we stumbled upon *Bridezillas*. I was like, *This is insane.* Jon and Maddie, the kids I nannied, told me they thought I could pull it off. I thought it was funny, so I jokingly sent an application. They called me the next day.

I have worked in media my entire adult life and have always looked at reality TV as not really reality. I assumed everybody else did the same. I was wrong. I did *Bridezillas*, and we played it up completely. There were a few real moments because it was sweatpants week (what I call my period) and I was emotional, but overall it was theatrics. It was also not my real wedding. My fiancé was from St. Lucia, so we got married on the island and then had a second ceremony in Minnesota, where I'm from. I just remember producers yelling at me multiple times because they said I was too funny, that I wasn't taking being a bridezilla seriously enough. I thought it would be an easy task. Acting crazy for nine days, for compensation, didn't seem so bad . . . but it was.

Being that person, even acting like that person, was beyond exhausting. I remember praying for people who actually lived that way. I was just acting and it was draining; there was no way they could be happy. It was absolutely miserable. When it was all said and done, I was so thankful. My friends and family got together to watch the premiere of the episodes. We laughed at the craziness, and I was glad it was over, but then the hate mail came. People were beyond mean. They wanted me dead. Seriously, dead over two thirty-minute episodes. I was confused. Sure, I was the person acting crazy, but the hate mail came from people who watch the show every week. How could they judge me, if that's their cup of tea? Despite the hate mail, the death threats, and horrible things said about my daughter, I still don't regret doing it. The people who know me, the people that matter, they know that girl never existed. The money we got from doing the show also helped pay for my father-in-law's funeral, and without *Bridezillas*, there would be no *Marriage Boot Camp*, and *Marriage Boot Camp* was life changing.

When I did *Marriage Boot Camp*, I did it for a few reasons. I really wanted the counseling for my postpartum depression, and I was feeling like I wanted to give up on my marriage. I also wanted to redeem myself for the nonsense that was *Bridezillas*. I remember along the way thinking, *God, I hope this helps*, and even questioning if I should do it. I have received thousands— literally thousands—of emails from couples thanking me and saying they appreciated our story, and women with postpartum depression looking for resources. When I read these messages, I know that show was bigger than my marriage issues. It was huge for me doing what I love most: helping people.

Marriage Boot Camp showed me glimpses of the person I

wanted to be. I believe that the twenty-one days that I stayed in that ten-million-dollar mansion really laid the foundation for the personal growth that I needed. I needed to let go of past hurt and learn to forgive. *MBC* forced me to evaluate the things that had contributed to my trust, abandonment, and intimacy issues. In short, the show taught me forgiveness. I dug deep, and I let go of the resentment I had toward my dad and the many other people who had a history of letting me down. More than anything else, though, *MBC* taught me to forgive myself. I can be really hard on myself. Afterward, I started giving myself permission to make mistakes.

When we headed back to actual reality, I honestly felt like we had made some serious strides. I had taken it very seriously and I wanted to come home and really put in the work. I wanted my marriage to last. I really did. But once we got home, I quickly realized that I wasn't the only one *MBC* gave permission to make mistakes.

Disloyalty

THIS IS THE hard part. This is where I tell you I was cheated on. Yes, me—the person with the awesome marriage. I was cheated on. This is also the part where I tell you that I stayed. Yes, me—the strong, outspoken, vibrant, intersectional feminist. I stayed with my cheating husband. I even had another baby with him.

Look, not every man is a cheater. At least, I hope not. But I will never, ever again marry a man who has access to a pussy buffet. No DJs, no basketball players, no musicians, no Tiger Woods. Seriously: Do. Not. Marry. Tiger. Woods.

I didn't marry Tiger Woods. I married a really good man. I adored him. He had spent two years wearing me down until I finally agreed to go on a date with him. He made me laugh until my face hurt. We laughed all the time. It was magical . . . until it wasn't.

I am not sure exactly when the shift happened. When the laughter turned into checking his cell phone, when the love turned to jealousy. You know the women who can crack any code? I became that woman. Seriously, I am a damn private eye. If you have a sneaking suspicion, trust, I can help you out.

Anyway, I digress. About three months before our beautiful Caribbean wedding, I had this feeling I couldn't shake. Always trust your gut. While he was half asleep, I told him my phone had died and I needed to call my mom. In reality, I had logged into his phone account online and told Verizon that he (I) had forgotten his password. Verizon then texted it to him (me), and I quickly deleted the Verizon text message and continued to discover all his sketchiness.

I did not tell him that I did this. Instead, I went to work and hatched my plan. While doing a midday radio show, I hopped on Gchat and started a conversation with my soon-to-be husband.

I told him that I had gotten an anonymous message from someone who said, "I hope you know who you are marrying . . ." If we are telling the truth here, I didn't get an anonymous message. I was my own tipster. I asked him if he had any idea why I would get a message like that.

He told me no, and I asked a few follow-up questions. It dawned on me that I probably was asking the wrong questions. So I revamped my line of questioning. Instead of asking him if he cheated on me, I asked him if he almost cheated on me. He responded . . . yes. Hold the hell on! Yes? How do you almost cheat on your soon-to-be wife? What exactly does almost mean? How the hell am I supposed to get back on the air after hearing this fuckery?

I didn't go back on the air. I walked into my boss's office and told him that I needed to go. There were tears streaming down my face, and he knew something horrible had happened. He attempted to pry a little bit, but I didn't have time for that. I needed to go home and channel my inner Angela Bassett in *Waiting to Exhale*.

On the way home, I called Best Friend Claire. I was not crying. I was very matter-of-fact. "Bitch, you got work to do," I said. "Go on ahead and start calling people. I mean, we can still go on vacation, but I'm not marrying his ass! Almost cheat on me, is he crazy?!" I don't even think I took a breath. "Look, I gotta get off the phone. I need to separate our bank accounts, get his ass off of my phone plan, and find his ass a place to stay." I am sure Claire said something amazing. She always does. She is the calm to my storm, always. I am sure she told me I would be okay. I am sure she said something profound. All I remember, though, is one sentence: "Just be sure of what you want to do, and of course, I got you."

Somehow, I got over it. Almost doesn't count, right? Oh, but it does. Almost is a huge red flag. Almost is an indicator of what is to come. Sometimes, almost hurts just as bad. I almost didn't marry him. Almost.

Three months later, I walked down the sandy aisle. I smiled and I looked amazing! I walked right into the arms of a man who had tears running down his face. It's an extremely beautiful moment to see a man cry because he is marrying you—until, for a brief moment, you think, *Oh shit, is he crying because he's marrying me?* Hello, self-doubt. You never fail me.

I spent seven years with this man. I know from the way it started you might think that it was all bad, but it wasn't. If it's possible for something to be beautifully painful, that was it. There were moments that I felt so loved. Moments when I felt he held me down like nobody else. There were moments that it was us against the world. There were moments when I saw forever and he was there.

There were also two perfect little girls. Equally me, equally him, and I loved every part of them. I especially loved the parts of them that were him. So yes, there were amazing moments, but that's all that they were: moments.

For a while, the moments got me through. We would have

these horrible periods of disconnection. I would want to run, pack up my heart and mind, and protect them from the isolation that was beginning to be my norm. But then a moment would happen. He would give me a little bit. He would give me that million-dollar smile, that incredible laugh that always made me laugh right along with him. He would make love to me, and I was right back at it. Ready to fight for us, ready to give my all to keep our family together. It was a vicious cycle.

I can't give you all the details of the day I found out he cheated on me. I will tell you that again I put my investigative skills to work and cracked his cell phone code. Fellas, come on, do better! I won't tell you what I found. Does it really matter? Yes, part of it is that I am embarrassed. But more so, if my daughters are gonna find out the details, they will find out directly from me. I am okay with my daughters knowing their father cheated on me. I am not okay with it changing their view of him.

It's a tough spot to be in. To want to tell your truth but also protect those that you love. For some reason that I will never understand, I even wanted to protect him. He was the father of my children.

When I handed him his cell phone, I took one of my favorite lines from *Brown Sugar*. "We got something to celebrate: our divorce."

When you realize that the reason your husband isn't connecting to you is that another woman has been getting all of his time and attention, there isn't much that can heal the pain that you feel. Staying in your walk-in closet for a few days watching Beyoncé's documentary on repeat will help protect your sanity, though.

I know he loved me. I'm not one of those people who think that if you cheat on someone you can't possibly love them. I'm not that naïve. This man loved the hell out of me. He still cheated. People don't cheat because there isn't love. (Well, some people do, but those people are assholes.)

My husband, who loved the hell out of me, cheated on me. I recognize that, and I live with that. I am now finally okay with that. We were amazing partners, almost like a business. When it came to our work and our kids, we were unstoppable. He is a good dad, but he was a terrible husband. I'm sure he thinks I was a terrible wife too. Somebody else will think he is a great husband, I am sure of it, and somebody will think I am the best wife on the planet, but we were not each other's person. I tried hard to be. Counseling, *Marriage Boot Camp*, another baby—none of that will save two people who are better at being a business deal than being friends and lovers.

I spent years feeling like a court jester. I changed so much of myself to suit his needs that I literally stopped recognizing who I was. I kept smiling, but I was dying on the inside. There was such a lack of consistency. One day he could make me laugh and kiss me passionately. I would grasp onto those moments and somehow conjure up hope. I wanted so bad for him to choose me. The real me—the not-perfect, super goofy, can't-cook-to-save-my-life-but-will-try-anyway me. I wanted to be good enough. I realize now that I spent the majority of my marriage feeling exactly the opposite.

The truth is, the cheating could have been forgiven. I loved him that much. I wanted our family to stay together. I wanted him. Feeling like I was being punished for his mistake, though, that is not forgivable. He cheated on me, and somehow it began to feel like it was my fault. He would claim everything was okay but would spend days in his man cave without talking to me. What hurt the most was that even after he cheated, I found him attractive. I wanted to make love to him, and he was just completely uninterested. So let me get this straight: you cheated on me, I forgave you, and now our marriage is devoid of intimacy? It made no damn sense. Still, I fought for us.

We became two ships passing in the night. The love that once encouraged me to fight for us turned to resentment. One night, I prayed like I had never prayed before. I begged the universe to help me, to help us. I guess I wasn't expecting to ever feel done. It happened, though; that help I was begging the universe for came. Rather than saving my marriage, the universe told me to save myself. The day after our precious second daughter was born, I felt something switch inside of me. She was born in October. In January, we went away for my birthday. It was enough time to heal from the delivery and to finally be intimate again. We were in a hotel, alone, and I was ready. But he didn't even try. I drank too much that trip. Alcohol masks the pain, but only temporarily. I celebrated my birthday and I smiled, but I knew. I knew I was done fighting for us. I was done trying to morph myself into someone he would love. I was done not having someone want to passionately make love to me, and I was done trying to prove that I was lovable, that I was worth it, that I wasn't invisible. I was done.

I came home from that trip, looked my best friend in the face, and said it out loud: "I don't want to be married anymore. I especially don't want to be married to him anymore." It took an entire year after that to speak those words out loud to anybody else, but finally the courage came and was stronger than the pain was deep, and I did it. I decided not to put any more faith into something that wasn't serving me. I decided to save my love for someone who wanted it. I chose to walk away before I hated him, because hate would be detrimental to our children. I chose freedom. I chose me. Easily the best decision I've ever made.

Divorce

AFTER SEVEN YEARS, two beautiful babies, tears, screams, and laughs, we signed on the dotted line and I got my daddy's last name back. I cried tears of sadness, and then relief. My best friend wrapped her arms around me as I wailed like a wounded animal. And then I opened my eyes and saw so many possibilities. I saw my new life. I felt apprehension, and I said to myself, *Self, you deserve happiness and love. Self, you deserve peace of mind.* So I packed up the fear, resentment, anger, disappointment, and self-doubt and mailed them off to ain't-nobody-got-time-for-that-land. I welcomed faith, truth, loyalty, love, adventure, self-discovery, and self-worth and told the universe I was ready. Ready to finally live up to my fullest potential. A calmness came over me, and I heard the universe speak to me:

"*And you will,*" she said.

I can't tell you how everyone reacts when they get a divorce, but I can tell you that I was a damn hot mess. When I got married, I really and truly believed that at the end of my life I would be old, still beautiful because black don't crack, and sitting in a rocking chair on a wrap-around porch. I would be holding the wrinkled hand of my beloved, who would also still be beautiful because black don't crack. I would beam with pride at my gorgeous grown daughters and snuggle with my grandbabies as much as possible. I would die and be mourned properly, and my beloved would die of a broken heart soon after. I'm talking like the next day or a few days after—straight *Where the Red Fern Grows* or *The Notebook* style. It would have been a beautiful life.

You know what happens when you plan your whole life out? Life happens, that's what. Life and I had drastically different versions of how my forever would look.

Co-parenting, splitting holidays, and therapy: that's what forever looks like to me right now. Not to mention the questions. There are so many questions!

—What do I do with my wedding ring?

—I look good in those wedding pictures—I was Beyoncé flawless that day—but now I just throw them away?

—Is it weird to keep family pictures? The girls should have those, right?

—Even though I do not want to be married to him, will it hurt when he gets into another relationship?

—Will it hurt him when I do?

—Does he miss our cat? Thank God he's not fighting me for cat custody.

—Did you know that people fight for animal custody?

Nonstop questions with no real answers. That's my forever right now.

The timeline of events went like this: Shit got bad. Shit got really bad. Shit could not be repaired. We filed for legal separation, he moved out, and I—well, I lost my damn mind. It was crazy beautiful; crazy because I was all over the place and beautiful because self-discovery was happening. I was finding myself.

Walking away from my marriage was hard. I loved him, I loved our family and our home, and I was obsessed with my version of forever. It wasn't real, though. None of it was real. I'm not sure if it ever was. I'd like to believe that at one point all of it was real, but remember, I questioned his tears as I walked down the aisle, so how real could it have been? As hard as it was, it was the right thing to do. And, honestly, divorce looks good on me. It looks good on him too. So many people see divorce as a scarlet letter, but not me. I wear my divorce like a badge of honor. When people tell me they are sorry about my marriage, I quickly tell them not to be. I'm not! Nobody said sorry when we were trapped in a marriage that was sucking the life out of both of us, so please don't say sorry now that we're free.

There's no handbook on how to do divorce. Actually, there might be. I bet if I googled it I would find something. It's probably on Amazon—and I have Prime, so I could get it in two days—but I'm not reading a damn book on divorce. Imagine me sipping my venti soy-milk chai tea latte at Starbucks and reading *How to Divorce for Dummies* on my Kindle, which I got in two days from Amazon Prime—yeah, I'll pass on that. I read all kinds of books on how to stay married and that didn't work, so I am doing divorce my way, and it's called Rumspringa.

Rumspringa

I MET JERSEY in a bar, and I was instantly drawn to him. We talked for hours, and I remember being so intrigued. We talked about everything, and it was just easy, natural. I remember thinking that he served a purpose. Even if I never saw him again, I realized that I could never be with someone who couldn't have conversations with me the way that he did. He leaned into the conversation. He was interesting and interested. He was smart as hell and funny. When he excused himself to use the bathroom, he put his hand on the small of my back, and as he walked away I remember thinking, *Who the hell is this guy? Where did he come from?*

The next day I met him for brunch. I sat across from this man and I listened. I'm a talker by nature and profession, so rarely does a person shut me up. I wanted to know his story and hear his truth. I wanted him to tell me all the things. The more he told me, the more I wanted to know. I was intrigued, and his energy was everything. He walked me to my car, and something unexpected happened. He told me that he understood the transition that I was going through with my job and divorce and that there was a book that helped him through it. He reached into his jacket, pulled out a book, and gave it to me.

Listen, I don't know if you've ever had a man give you a book, but in that moment it's hard to keep it together. I instantly heard

Ginuwine's "Pony" in my mind and thought, *Oh, he can get it.* I kid you not. Jersey was smooth as hell.

About a week later, Jersey took me out in New York. We ate the best Hispanic food I have ever had, and again the conversation did not disappoint. I was feeling Jersey. After dinner, Jersey took me to a pub down the street. We posted up in this very intimate booth. Again he wrapped me into his conversation. At one point I realized I didn't know what the hell he was saying. I remember thinking that there was no way I was that drunk. I wasn't. I was daydreaming. His words disappeared. I saw his lips moving and I knew he was talking that good talk, but I heard nothing. Jersey paused midsentence. I was sure he was saying something fascinating, but as he took a breath I blurted out, "Can I kiss you?" He slid over in the booth and passionately kissed me. I sank my whole body into his, thinking, *What is he doing to me? Who knew mental stimulation could be so sexy?* He asked me to meet him in Chicago and I breathlessly told him, "I'll do my best." He walked me back to the Airbnb that I was staying at. My mind was blown. He was a man, a real man. Real men have amazing conversations. They talk about real shit. I've been surrounded by boys, so this—this was a whole new world.

A few weeks later, I walked into a Chicago hotel and grabbed the key he left for me at the front desk. I had trouble breathing in the elevator. I couldn't figure out if the corset under my sweater dress was too tight or if I was having a panic attack.

Get it together, Danielle. You are a grown-up! I pulled it together and I let myself into the room. Jersey was brushing his teeth, shirtless. My breathing picked up. Damn corset! I figured it was coming off soon, though, so I sucked it up.

When I turned around, he was looking at me. I hugged him and he pushed me into the wall. I've never really been dominated, but if he was gonna Christian Grey me, I wasn't gonna put up a fight. I spent five years in a marriage begging for intimacy like this. I was along for the ride. Sweater dress was over my head and corset was off quickly. This was my after-baby body, so I was a little self-conscious, but he wasn't looking for, or at, stretch marks. He threw me on the bed and I gave in to all of it. I told him not to stop, and he locked eyes with me and said, "Don't tell me what to do." Ohhhhhh. I didn't tell him anything after that. He took control, and I let him. It crossed my mind that I didn't tell him a safe word—there I go, always looking for an exit strategy—but it didn't seem like the right moment to bring it up, so I went with it. Afterward, he held me and rubbed my back and ran his hands through my hair. Listen, I have naturally curly hair. It's a process to run your fingers through it, but he did it effortlessly. I was impressed! All that playing with my hair made me look like a member of the Jackson 5, but it was worth the time it took to comb it out.

Jersey took me to an exquisite dinner, a blues club, and then back to the hotel for more rounds of domination. Rumspringa was off to a great start. I liked him. Our energy matched. We laid in bed for hours talking about Prince. He told me his dreams and fears, and his ambition was everything. I felt like I had known him for forever. I was happy to have met him. He sparked something inside of me that I didn't even know existed. I'm glad it did.

While in the Chi, I visited my friend Angi. She took me to this classy restaurant. It was like an episode of *Sex and the City*. We were fancy as hell that day. We discussed being women in radio and what that atmosphere was like for us, and we drank and had a blast.

As we walked back to the car, we passed a Louboutin store. Angi insisted that I go in and get myself a pair. She told me I deserved it. She was convincing as hell, but I couldn't even pronounce the name of the shoe. What the hell would I look like walking around in red bottoms? The peer pressure was real, though, so I went in to take a peek.

Let me give you some advice: do not walk into a Louboutin store to window-shop. I dare you to try to leave the store without buying something. If you try it and make it out alive, let me know how the hell you pulled that off!

I was in the store, trying on shoes, and the sales associates were good—like, really good. They had me in there thinking I could really afford that shit. I realized the only way out was to make a purchase. I had no intention of ever wearing the pair I chose, and since I knew I was going to return these beautiful, ridiculously priced shoes, I wasn't really worried about the cost. I swiped my credit card and got the hell out.

I'll be the first to tell you it was irrational, buying a pair of shoes just to get out of a store, but I did it, and I kept those bad boys in the box. I was afraid that even looking at them would inhibit the return process.

If you own Louboutins, more power to you. If you bought them for yourself—go 'head, baller. If someone bought them for you—yaaass. You know why you shouldn't own Louboutins? You shouldn't own Louboutins because you bought a pair just to get out of the store quickly with the intention of returning them, only to discover that Louboutin doesn't accept returns.

So I own a pair of Louboutins by default—or stupidity, however you want to look at it. Either way, I took those bad boys out of the box, put them on my feet, and holy hell did they look good. I won't lie, when I am wearing them they make me feel like a new woman. But once I realized that my new red bottoms could have easily been two Broadway tickets to see Lin-Manuel Miranda in *Hamilton*, I was back on team Fuck Louboutin.

Jersey and I fell off. It was really me just realizing that, as amazing as he was, it would never work. And just like that, our whirlwind romance ended.

Detroit was special. He was always special. He was one of my best friends. We had an interesting relationship. As a teenager, he taught me sex education. He was much more experienced than the rest of us, and he filled in all the blanks. Because of him, I take hooker baths to this day when I am in a hurry. On one of his visits home from the military, he gave me his dog tag. That was a terrible idea because I lose everything, but over a decade later it's still one of my most prized possessions and I know exactly where it is. It's mind-blowing, really.

After a divorce, sex is scary. I had been with the same person for seven years, and we had sex sparingly. I had no idea what the kids were doing now. I was told that ladies weren't even matching panties and bras anymore, and I was like, WTF? Jumping back into sex world wasn't gonna to be easy.

I called Detroit and told him my predicament. I told him that I needed a safe space to try out sex. I told him that he was my safe space. In retrospect, I realize that what I was saying was, "Hey, you are so friend-zoned for life, so just let me use you for sex so I can get back into the game." But at the time, I was shocked when he was hesitant. He told me that our friendship was special and sleeping together might complicate that. I told him it was us and we would be all right. He reluctantly agreed.

I geared up for our sex date, and then something weird happened. I realized that I couldn't just have sex with Detroit. I loved him. I loved him on a level that was so deep that there was no way it would only be sex. So I told him and took him out of the friend zone. A few weird dates turned into a few amazing dates and really good sex. It also led to one of my most embarrassing sexual situations.

Detroit was home from grad school, so he was bunking on a cot in the living room at his dad's, Papa J. One night, we met up with a group of our high school friends and drank. I mean, we drank a lot. We may have drank so much that, at six in the morning, Detroit smacked me on my bare-naked ass and told me to get up because we couldn't be laying on the cot in the middle of the living room like this. He got up to investigate, and I quickly threw on a pair of oversized basketball shorts. I was giggling to myself because, yes, this sucked, but at least we woke up before anyone else. Wrong. Detroit comes back into the living room only to tell me that Papa J. had already left for his morning walk. Not a big deal, except he had to walk right by us and all our nakedness to get to the front door.

Later that day, while Detroit was at work, Papa J. and I went to see *Finding Dory*. It could have been massively embarrassing—after all, he did see all my goodies—but, like a true gentleman, he never said a word.

Rumspringa was in full effect. Detroit and I had an understanding. We loved each other, but we were also in no position to settle down. So we continued to see each other but also didn't police each other's extracurriculars. I was doing my thing, and he was doing his.

Minneapolis was home. He was all things home. We had been connected since we were kids. He had always been my friend, checking up on me over the years. Out of nowhere, he reached out because, of course, Universe, I needed more shit to juggle. We went on a walk, and my entire body felt different when I was around him. He was kryptonite. Loving Minneapolis was easy because, like I said, he was home. He was comfortable. He came from where I came from. When he touched me, my whole body reacted. He was smart, kind, and an empath. I had never been intimately connected to someone who was so much like me. I really should have paid attention, but I was blinded by the way my body felt when I was with him. He could look at me and send shivers down my spine. He was mostly accessible at night, though, and that should have been the first red flag. I joked with him that I was his nighttime girlfriend and that I knew he had a daytime girl.

Sometimes jokes are rooted in truth. The mother of his son called me, and when we traded stories, we realized that we had been living like sister-wives. So I invited her over to my house and we FaceTimed him together. The look on his face was price-less, and for a second I felt like it was exactly what he deserved, but honestly nobody won. She discovered the father of her child cheated, I discovered my lifelong friend was living a double life and I was involved in it, and he lost all the way around. Rumspringa was complicated.

It wouldn't be right to tell the story of Rumspringa without giving a special shoutout to North Carolina. He was the first man I slept with after being with my husband for seven years. I couldn't bring myself to have practice sex with Detroit after I realized the love I had for him, so we avoided it and I dated around. North Carolina was sexy. He had the most intense voice ever. I've been a radio personality for my entire adult life, so when I hear a great voice, I notice. North Carolina will always be special because he taught me that I wasn't sexually broken. For so long I had so many questions. I wondered why my husband didn't want me. Didn't men want sex all the time? Was I not good at it? Did he not find me attractive anymore? It's a horrible space to be in to constantly question why the one person who is supposed to want you doesn't. I needed someone to want me. I had spent entirely too long not being wanted.

North Carolina wanted me. It was obvious, and he was a damn magician. We walked into his apartment, and by the time we were in his bedroom he had all of my clothes off. I didn't even see it coming. It was amazing sex. I remember wanting to cry. I wasn't broken. I was far from broken. I was sexual. I loved sex. I wanted it, and after what I had been through, I deserved it. Honestly, North Carolina was probably the catalyst for Rumspringa. I will forever be in debt to him and his phenomenal sex.

Rumspringa was full of beautiful chaos. It was the time I took to really get to know myself, and a few others, sexually. Back in the day, Claire and I had this dumb-ass pact to sleep with five or fewer people because, you know, our husbands wouldn't want us if we slept with more. I'm not sure what the hell we were thinking. I don't even remember anyone putting the fear of God into us. I literally think we just made the pact and that was that. I followed the pact except for one oops, but—for reasons I could write an entire book on—he doesn't count. Years later, Claire would call me and break the pact. She wasn't married and I was, but still I was all, "Bitch, a pact is a pact!" She told me she had anticipated being married by then and since she wasn't, she went off and had a mini Rumspringa of her own. I lived vicariously through her. God bless her.

Rumspringa gave me a confidence that I had never had sexually. I controlled my body, and I learned how to use it. If I wanted sex, I got it. With everything else kind of out of control in my life, sex made me feel good and even gave me a sense of power. I had never had a one-night stand pre-Rumspringa. I wasn't really spontaneous. Every man that I had ever been with had been someone I loved or cared deeply for.

But this was Rumspringa. I was mending my broken heart, and my vagina was low on miles in comparison to everyone else I knew. So I texted an extremely successful associate of mine and I told him I wanted to be on his desk. I giggled like a damn kid, but liquid courage was making me bold. I was flying from DC to Minneapolis and didn't get in until almost midnight, but when I landed I wanted to go to his office and have sex on his desk.

When he agreed, I realized I was not dressed appropriately for the fantasy to play out smoothly. I was wearing jeans, long socks, and boots. I could just see myself struggling to get my tight-ass pants off, and I couldn't have that. My friend Christie and I headed to LOFT to remedy the situation. The sales rep found me a sweater dress that matched my boots and socks. When the cashier told me that LOFT didn't sell panties, Christie and I said in unison, "Just take 'um off."

A few hours later, I landed in Minneapolis and headed to his office. I played it much cooler than I felt. He led me into his office and wasted no time. I first noticed that he was a great kisser. For me, kissing compatibility is a necessity. He smelled really good, and he had me on his desk. I quickly checked that off my bucket list. The movies make having sex on a desk much sexier than it really is. Don't get me wrong, the sex was nice, but it wasn't comfortable at all. Still, the experience was worth it. I still feel bad that my fantasy led to his back hurting, but it was fun. Afterward, I sat at his desk, in his chair, and asked him many questions about his high-profile job. I was new to sporadic random sex, so I felt like it was the right thing to do.

I wasn't really ready to wrap up Rumspringa, but then Mr. Magic showed up. Mr. Magic was great on paper. Great job, loved God, was a good dad. He made me laugh, and we had fun together. He supported my social activism, noticed my eyebrows, and saw me as the unicorn that I am. I was smitten. We had a whirlwind romance. We traveled to Sacred Stone and joined the #NoDAPL protests, perused the JFK memorial in Dallas, and spent my birthday weekend in Orlando visiting Disney World and attending the Pro Bowl. I was really enjoying myself. Oh, and the sex was great. Like, really great.

It could have worked. I really liked him, but I started to pull away and distance myself. My therapist, Beth—who is a saint, by the way—asked me if I was self-sabotaging. I had wondered that too, but this was different. I had started having flashbacks to my marriage, and they were all good memories. I knew I didn't want to be with my ex, so why was I reminiscing? I had spent so much time being angry that I had forgotten that we had shared some amazing moments. They flooded my mind. I remembered the laughter, the Michael Bublé serenades, the silly dance offs we would have. I remembered being a family, and this overwhelming feeling of loss washed over me. I realized that, as fun as Rumspringa was, it was a distraction. I spent a year masking my hurt with sex, wine, and eventually Mr. Magic. It was time to face the pain. It was time to mourn, and it was something I needed to do on my own. So I walked away from Mr. Magic and allowed myself to mourn the end of a seven-year love story. A story that was both ugly and beautiful. Quite the paradox.

Mourning is interesting. I go from wanting to be really cordial to my ex for the sake of our daughters and because I still have so much love for him to literally wanting to physically harm him because it still hurts. Sometimes I say really mean things, things that he deserves to hear but that only make me feel worse. Sometimes I cry randomly. Sometimes I laugh randomly. Sometimes I don't want to feel anything, but I continue on because I have to. I have two amazing little girls counting on me.

Him

I PUT HIS name in my cell phone as "Him." Referring to him that way was the only thing that really made sense. He was like this mythical creature, the great white buffalo—you know, the one that got away. For years we had been friends, great friends, but there was never any denying that we had chemistry. We had all the chemistry, and after my divorce and his break-up, it seemed like finally after all of these years the timing was right. It wasn't. I was ready to make him a choice. He was ready to keep me as an option. It shouldn't have been surprising; he had this way of popping in and out of my life. He'd done it for years. I just assumed we weren't together because timing was always wrong. After I decided to choose him, choose us, I quickly realized that he saw me as someone he could always come back to. A good option to always have on deck but not necessarily one he would ever choose.

There's so much to say about this. There were the best kisses ever, one good night of sex, years of friendship, and disappointment. I went into this essay wanting to recount every detail, wanting to make sense of it all, but something better happened. The details don't matter as much as the lesson. Him was a season person who I allowed to occupy lifetime space. Epiphany. I love when that happens. In this case, it happened much later than

I hoped it would. Nevertheless, it happened. I had some great times with Him, but I should have seen earlier on that he wasn't ready for my loyalty, love, and friendship.

The hurt has subsided some, but the lesson is ingrained on my spirit. We gotta stop letting season people occupy lifetime space. Sometimes it's important to tighten up your circle. If people don't make you a choice, don't be their option. I started doing just that, and the results have been empowering. I distanced myself from Him and other people who weren't worthy of lifetime benefits. Can I be petty for a moment? Since we've already established that season people don't deserve lifetime perks, they probably don't deserve long essays in your book either . . . so, moving on.

I'm Not Perfect!

I GET LETTERS all the time telling me that I am an inspiration, that somehow my words or actions have made an impact on the lives of strangers. I appreciate that so much. I want to do good, in this world and for this world. I'm not perfect, though. I am as flawed as can be. I have done some shitty things, some things that I am not proud of. It's all a part of growth.

I tried for years to master perfection. I was never good at it, but still I tried. Trying to obtain perfection is a lost cause, let me tell you. When I get these amazing letters from people, it feels like I'm doing something right, but it's also a good time to remind myself that I can be an asshole too. I am human. I even keep a list of shitty things I've done just so I don't ever get too high and mighty.

I once punched my brother in the eye. I cried with him afterward, but still, I punched my baby brother in the eye. We had to lie about it because obviously he couldn't go to school and say his sister beat him up. I still feel bad about it.

I cheated on my high school sweetheart and didn't tell him until college. I loved him too, really loved him. I still love him.

I remember seeing a girl at the mall who I didn't recognize. She recognized me and asked me if I still hung out with my friends Nikki and Cheri. I told her, of course, that they were like my family. She replied, "Oh, you guys were so mean to me." I was a bully and I don't even remember it. This one sticks with me. I didn't remember doing something and that something I did stayed with a person for years.

As a kid, I would steal hair clips from Brookdale Mall. I would walk in, unclip them from the package, stick them in my mouth, and walk out. Not only is that stupid, but it's also just plain unsanitary.

I was terrible to my friend Jackie. I was depressed and battling postpartum depression, and she was an easy target. She was beautiful and happy all the time, and I was miserable and couldn't function. I hated myself, and so I hated her and hated on her. I am beyond thankful that she has a forgiving heart.

Sometimes I accidentally dream about my friend's husband. I can't help it! One, it's a dream, which I can't control, and two, he looks like Fitz from *Scandal* . . . I'm sorry, Mary Clare.

I cheated on tests a few times in high school.

I lied to my parents about being sexually active.

I smoked weed.

I texted and drove way too many times.

I am not perfect. The good thing is that, when I began to truly love myself, I started to embrace my imperfections. I am a constant work in progress. I am not the final version of myself, and I won't ever be until the day I die. Every day is a new day for more self-work and more personal growth. I am not who I used to be, and I know the mistakes I have made along the way have played a major role in my progression as a person. I'm not perfect, and that's just fine with me.

You're Beautiful

I WAS SIXTEEN years old and in love with a boy who was heading to the military. We didn't have much time left together, as he was soon headed off to basic training. I was sitting at the living room table applying makeup, getting ready for one of our date nights. In walks this blond-haired, blue-eyed, inquisitive little three-year-old. (Genetics are a trip.)

"What are you doing?" he asked in the cutest voice ever.

"I'm putting on makeup."

"But why?"

At this point I was annoyed. I mean, hello, I was sixteen and I didn't really have the time to talk to my three-year-old little brother.

"Because it makes me pretty."

His face instantly changed, and he looked a little sad. He turned around and headed out of the room. As he got to the door, he paused, back still turned to me. He sighed very dramatically and shrugged his shoulders. He shook his little head back and forth . . .

"She doesn't know she's beautiful," he said, and he walked out of the room.

My annoyed sixteen-year-old self sat there stunned. How did this little three-year-old just melt my heart? How was he capable of making me feel so much so quickly?

Fourteen years later . . .

We were on our way to the National Harbor, and I was putting on a little bit of makeup in the backseat. A cocky seventeen-year-old sat in the front passenger seat while Slim drove. Munch was watching me, and she asked to put on some of my makeup. I instantly told her that she didn't need makeup. She whined a little and said that she didn't feel pretty enough. I felt like someone gut punched me. We had this talk about her heart and being a good person and the fact that makeup isn't needed for her to feel good; she's a good person and has an amazing spirit.

The cocky seventeen-year-old spoke up from the front seat. "You're beautiful, seriously!"

I told Munch, "See, even Uncle Sammy thinks you're beautiful!"

"I do," he said, "but I was talking to you, Danielle."

It instantly took me back to the conversation we had so long ago. His blond hair had since turned brown, and some days I wanted to choke him out because he was seventeen and knew everything, but some things remained the same: those beautiful blue eyes and the fact that, when he told me I was beautiful, I believed him. I love you, little brother! Thank you!

Broad Squad

IT HAD BEEN way too long. I missed my broad squad, and it was about time we had a reunion. Kiley took charge because that was her role within our squad. She's a take-charge, super type-A, gotta-get-shit-done kind of girl. My initial idea was for the five of us to get rid of all outside distractions. I wanted to be with my girls in a tree house. It seemed like a great idea. We would leave behind the stresses of marriages, kids, and jobs, and we would drink, explore nature, and camp out in a tree house. I was so damn geeked that I could barely contain my excitement. I thought my idea was foolproof, and it might have been, but it wasn't Kiley-proof. Somehow, despite my best attempts at getting these broads to disconnect and bunk with me in a tree house, Kiley planned an entirely different vacation. So there I was, on a plane headed to Colorado. I know what you're thinking: Did she at least find us a tree house in Colorado? Nope! But, to her credit, Kiley did find us one hell of an Airbnb, and it was one of my favorite trips ever. Kiley's a bossy bitch, and we love her for it.

We were talking over each other, excitedly trying to fill each other in on the things that we'd missed. We were taking trips down memory lane. We reminisced about the friend who gave me a five-dollar gift card as a wedding present. Mary Clare was laughing hysterically. She couldn't fathom that this was real life, but it was. We really had a friend who gave me a five-dollar gift card, but hey, it's the thought that counts, right? No! My friend was bogus as hell. Don't get me wrong—I didn't need her ass to get me a KitchenAid mixer, but come the hell on. The truth is, it wasn't that big of a deal, but I can tell a story like no other and Mary Clare had tears rolling down her face, so I continued on with my shenanigans.

At this point, I was trying to convince Mary Clare that she should stop laughing, because she didn't get me anything. She wasn't having it, though. She literally wracked her brain trying to remember what she got me years ago. It didn't matter, but it was hilarious watching her. She even wanted to check her bank statement. Mary Clare is probably everyone's favorite. Now, we have never talked about this, but just as parents have a favorite kid—thanks, Dad—our broad squad MVP is Mary Clare.

Linnea was pregnant with a baby whose gender she didn't know. We all wanted to know what she was carrying, but she was making everybody wait. In all fairness, she was waiting too, but we wanted to know! Linnea is laid back. Shit literally rolls off her. It's really hard for me to recall a time when she's lost it or wasn't even-keel. She's no drama, literally no drama. If you don't have one of those in your squad, let me tell you now that you need one. It didn't surprise us one bit that Linnea wanted her baby's gender to be a surprise. If Mary Clare is everyone's favorite, Linnea is the one that nobody really has to worry about. She's usually all good.

Claire was talking to Kiley about how we were splitting everything on the trip. Kiley insisted that we put everything on her credit card and then she would tally and send us bills. Yep, that's our Kiley. Claire was navigating us to the nearest liquor store. This was probably not a great idea because Claire can't navigate for shit. To be clear, Claire can't navigate the road. She can, however, navigate in the most beautiful of ways, showing up in an instant whenever any of us need her.

When MC moved to NY, Claire went often. When Kiley moved to Chicago, Claire went often. After Linnea's epic barn wedding, Claire spent hours cleaning up. And when it comes to me, well, Claire is my person. We met when I was twelve and she was thirteen, and since then we have been each other's ride-or-die! I love her so much that I dedicated an entire essay to her in this book.

My role in our broad squad is simple. First, I am the token black. Most importantly, though, I bring the funny! I am pure comic relief, and I love that they have been laughing at my jokes for over a decade. As individuals, we are strong, independent women. But as a group, we are a force, a sisterhood, a tribe. They are my tribe.

The five of us have seen each other through everything. A cheating husband, the death of a significant other, the births of children, fertility issues, multiple divorces, illnesses, etc. Denver was special because it allowed us to disconnect from the real world and act like the younger, unmarried, non-mother versions of ourselves. Denver also had legalized marijuana.

Colorado wasn't all edibles and shenanigans, though. On this trip, I sat across from my broad squad and I asked, "What should I do?" (regarding my marriage and, you know, the rest of my life). Broad squad went dark on me, pure silence, crickets— loud-ass crickets. It was weird because before they would always chime in, stay strong, fight harder, push through. Not this time. Silence. Their silence said so much. When your entire squad opts out of telling you to continue to fight for your marriage, it's time to dig deep and ask yourself the tough questions.

Best Friend Claire

"I KNOW THIS probably sounds weird because, understandably, you're stressed and everything seems uncertain right now, but I am so excited for you. Like, I feel like I'm going to explode. Yes, it's scary, and I'm sorry you're going through this, and I'm actually enraged for you. But I have such a good feeling. You are on the cusp of something amazing. We just don't know what it looks like yet. I've been praying for discernment for you every day, in every avenue of your life. When the path isn't clear, sometimes a little light helps. I am sending all my light to you, and I know brighter days are ahead. Keep faith, and when you don't know what to do, just let go and trust everything will work out. It will be greater and better. Shit might get rough, but just know that if you didn't have a penny to your name, you and the girls would be taken care of. You never have to worry. I know that won't happen, but just remember that's what is most important, and you can let go of all of the other bullshit. If something doesn't serve you, it isn't for you. I know you will discover what is for you, and I can't wait to see what it looks like. I love you."
—BFC

When I was fourteen I wrote a poem for my best friend. As I was moving, I stumbled onto it and realized that it remains true. It made me extremely happy! Here's to the best relationship I have ever had and to poems that stay true decades later.

IF...
If the oceans dried up and the stars fell from the sky, you would hold my hand so I would never cry.

And if the trees fell over and the flowers never grew, I would never worry because I would have you.

And if the birds stopped singing and the sky was never blue, I would call your name and you would know what to do.

And if the sun stopped burning and the world would surely end, my life would have great meaning because you were my friend.

Sometimes people ask me how I got through some of the things that have happened to me. I know a lot of it was my own strength and pure determination. I would be lying, however, if I said I did it alone. I haven't had to go through any hardship alone since I was in middle school.

The story of how we met is interesting. Years ago, one of us was drowning in the falls at Webber Park in Minneapolis. One of us then grabbed a huge stick and pulled the other to safety. For years, we told the story that it was me who had been drowning, but Claire recently found her old journal, and the story in it is exactly the same except that she was the one who was drowning and I saved her. We are not sure at all how the story changed over the years, but it makes sense.

Claire is a lifesaver—literally. She works in a pediatric ICU, and she saves lives daily. Saving lives and nursing people back to health isn't just her job; it is her calling and life's work. When our friend Tessa got into a terrible skiing accident, Claire was right there as her own personal nurse. When our friend Evan fell off a train platform and broke something in his leg, Claire helped nurse him back to health. When her cousin had the misfortune of colliding with a bus while biking, Claire was there to help in any way possible. That's probably why we remember her being the saver in the drowning story. Honestly, even if it was me that saved her life, she's been saving my life ever since, so we're even.

Claire rejuvenates my soul on every level. This is a woman who took doula classes to make sure that I had a better experience giving birth the second time around. (She was there to witness it the first time, and she fully understood how badly I was yearning for a different outcome.) When I told her I was interested in hypnobirthing classes but couldn't believe how expensive they were, she paid half. When my midwife let me know that I could choose who actually caught my baby and handed her to me (husband opted out), I asked Claire if she would do the honors. She cried, which was a huge deal because Claire is not a crier at all.

She is quite possibly the only reason I survived postpartum depression, because she refused to let me fall deeper into nothingness. And, because I was scared about it the second time around, she took the entire month of October off to help me deliver my baby and to watch me postpartum. She FaceTimes my daughters at least a few times a week and, despite not seeing each other face to face very often, Munchie and Smoochie know Claire better than anyone else. She sponsored my wedding cakes (all ten of those awesome Patty Cakes), held my hand the entire night before I got married, and held me as I cried the day I signed my divorce papers. I am eternally thankful for her.

Nobody—and I mean nobody—knows my spirit, my heart, or my mind the way that she does. She has truly been my rock.

I only hope that I am to her what she is to me. I am a faith-filled person, but sometimes I doubt God. Doubting often leads to greater faith, though, so I just go with it. I don't know what I did to deserve someone like her, but I am thankful daily and I don't doubt that it was on purpose. God knew I needed her, and I did. I do. Side note: My best friend is so humble that this will embarrass the hell out of her, but I don't care. She is the greatest human I've ever known, and I'm telling everybody.

I used to think that I couldn't survive without Claire. I admit, I have been a little codependent on her at times. She has been my security blanket. For so long, I attributed my survival to her, and honestly she ensured my survival on many occasions, so I was okay with that. I didn't realize that finding that same trust in myself was possible. That being my own ride-or-die could be life-changing, that I could be my own Claire and that she could be my safety net. I didn't realize I needed to have in myself that same unwavering faith I had in her.

Finding the strength to walk away from my marriage and making it through the bullshit misogyny and sexism I experienced in my career forced me to see my own strength, and it's been beautiful. When I began to love myself, everything around me transformed. It was like people saw that I was self-assured and fed off my energy and then gave me back that same positive energy. Wonderful things started happening. Life started happening. I felt alive. I was finally living authentically.

The Future Is Female

"And since we all came from a woman
Got our name from a woman and our game from a woman
I wonder why we take from our women
Why we rape our women, do we hate our women?
I think it's time to kill for our women
Time to heal our women, be real to our women."

—Tupac

IT'S HARD BEING a woman. If you are a woman, I probably don't have to tell you. If you are a smart man, I probably don't have to tell you that either. Periods, birth, unequal pay, terrible maternity leave, male-dominated workplaces—male privilege is real.

I often think of how society has taught us how we are supposed to behave as women. It's shoved down our throats from the time that we are little. Cross your legs, don't climb trees, don't say that, science isn't for you, don't do that, don't be that, don't wear that, don't be loud, and smile more, sweetheart. Who I am supposed to be as a woman is decided for me, and if I take the road less traveled, there just might be hell to pay.

I wonder how we as women feel valued when we live in a world where old men get to decide what we are allowed to do with our bodies. Where we are slut-shamed for owning our sexuality but men are applauded for adding another notch on their belts. Where our passion is often confused with aggression and we can be doing the same job as a male coworker and even be better at it but still be paid less.

I walked into a male-dominated industry at the age of nineteen. I was smart, passionate, hardworking, and determined, but I was always first complimented on my looks and not my work ethic. I didn't choose to look the way that I do, but I did choose to bust my ass in college. I did choose to take an unpaid internship. I did choose to spend hours studying. It's like none of that mattered.

I've worked with men who were overweight and men who did not always smell good. Nobody ever said anything to them. If I put on a few pounds, it was not only noticed, but it was also spoken on. My coworker literally smelled like shit, but my five-pound fluctuation needed an intervention.

I once had a male coworker bust into the studio that I was working in and say, "Danni Starr, every time you come around, I just gotta get my dick sucked." When my manager questioned why he would say such a thing, he said that he was just singing lyrics to a song, as if DMX's "Party Up" included my name and as if that were even a logical reason.

That coworker later sexually assaulted me in the dark backroom of our workplace. I wonder what song told him to do that. In his defense, I probably had it coming. Maybe I smiled at him a little too long or wore something a little too tight. Maybe I shouldn't have been in that dark room alone—or maybe, when a woman is sexually assaulted, she shouldn't be put on trial. Maybe it doesn't matter what she wore, where she was, or if she was nice. Maybe if a man decided to push her up against a wall with his hot-ass breath against her skin and attempted to tell her that she wanted it, maybe it was his fault. Wait, there's no maybe: it is his fault.

It's tough being a woman. We live in a world where we are blamed for our sexual assaults, where often the impact of the punishment of the rapist is considered more than the impact of the rape on the victim. It's tough being a woman.

You know what the worst part is? I'm not so sure my co-worker even thought he was doing something wrong. After all, ever since he was little, he's been groomed to know and believe that women are second-class citizens, that his rights are more important than mine, that he is a part of the stronger, smarter gender.

Remembering London

WHEN I GOT back from London, I literally felt like I had gained a new perspective. I was ready to conquer all aspects of my existence. My new, vastly different life—my no-husband, no-job, single-momma life. I was ready and I felt unstoppable, but I wasn't. Losing my forever was initially a relief. I knew it was the right thing, and I knew we would all be better off. I knew I would flourish. What I didn't expect was to miss him. The thing is, I didn't miss us. I don't even think it was him that I was missing. I missed the idea of my forever. I was lonely. I was lonely while I was married to him, but this loneliness was different. Even though he wasn't really present in our marriage, he was still around, still present in our home. He had been emotionally gone for a long time, but now he was physically gone and I was lonely.

When my radio career abruptly came to a halt, I was strong-willed and initially didn't allow the disappointment to drag me into a dark place. Yes, it sucked, but after it ended amazing things happened to me and for me. Huge opportunities landed at my feet, and not only did I accept them, but I slayed! The TLC network signed me to a better deal and flew me out to work on the set of a Tyler Perry show.

Here I was, professionally killing it. When I am working, I am in my zone. I have no doubt that I am great at what I do. It's when I come home, when I tuck the girls in their beds and I am alone in my thoughts, that pieces of my sanity start to crumble. That's when I remember that I'm lonely. I'm in need of adult interaction. I spend the majority of my time taking care of little humans who have zero appreciation for the sacrifices I've made for them, and I'm okay with it because they are little humans who can't really comprehend that. But I wipe other people's asses every day. I read the same books repeatedly. I have had a kid that I pushed out of my vagina tell me that I broke her heart because she couldn't play on her tablet. I've spent too much time explaining that you shouldn't bite your sister, growl at your sister, or take your diaper off and smear your shit everywhere. Like, seriously, WTF is up with that? I love my kids, but toddlers can be assholes and I need real adult interaction.

At night, when I'm tucked into my bed with a glass of Hogue Late Harvest Riesling, Netflix and chillin' with my damn self, that's when I remember how hard it is being a woman in a male-dominated industry and that I'm lonely.

Loneliness and disloyalty, that's what made me forget London. That's what brought me back into the Darkness. I guess if I am telling you that I went back into the Darkness, I have to explain to you how I got there in the first place.

Step into the Darkness: Postpartum Depression and Anxiety

ON JUNE 22, 2016, I stood at a podium on Capitol Hill and gave a speech on my experience with postpartum depression and anxiety, aka PPD/PPA, aka the Darkness.

"Once upon a time I knew a woman. She was fearless, confident. I mean, she could stand next to Halle Berry and still feel beautiful. She was a powerhouse. She had a beautiful wedding and shortly after got pregnant. She was thrilled. She had always wanted to be a mom. After the birth of her daughter, she felt emotions she had never felt before with such severity. She was paranoid, irritable, angry, irrational, sad. She didn't eat or sleep. She quickly became a shell of the person that she used to be. Her paranoia caused her to kidnap her own child, to go on the run for fourteen days, to believe that her best friend in the entire world was trying to have an affair with her husband, to count enough sleeping pills to knock her out for a few days but hopefully not kill her.

"She suffered, she left her job, her marriage crumbled. Every part of her life suffered. She was a woman who would do anything to help anybody, who was in trouble, yet she couldn't even recognize her own struggle.

"She had postpartum depression, something that she had never heard of despite the fact that she had taken every baby class possible and read a million books. Nothing and no one told her to protect her mental health.

"I knew her very well. She was amazing! But she doesn't exist anymore. She didn't die—although I can tell you that she wouldn't have been disappointed if she had—but still, she doesn't exist. Postpartum depression changed her to her core.

"When she had her second baby, she was happy and so excited because she just knew that she didn't have PPD, but she had horrible intrusive thoughts. She envisioned her children's deaths. She buried literally every person that she loved in her mind. She planned escape routes in every situation. She had to sit facing an exit, kept sharp objects in her car—you know, just in case she went over a bridge, landed in water, and needed to break a window to survive. She had no idea that PPD had an evil stepsister—postpartum anxiety.

"She was amazing! She had babies, her mind failed her, and then the medical field failed her, and government policies too, and she will never be the same. I can tell you this with certainty because I used to know her. I actually used to be her.

"I'm Danni, and I am a postpartum depression and anxiety survivor. It was the scariest, most awful time of my life, and I am not who I used to be. I had to find a new normal.

"I remember hearing and seeing stories of women who had killed their babies and thinking, *Wow, there's a special place in hell for them.* Perspective is everything, though, because a few months after my daughter was born, I remember thinking, *Thank God she is not a crier because, if she was, I'd probably kill us both.* Those women shouldn't burn in hell. Those women were living in hell on earth! Their minds, emotions, and rationality turned against them, and they needed help! They needed someone to tell them that what they were going through was actually the most common side effect of childbirth. They needed to be screened. They needed laws in place to protect them and their babies.

"They needed to know that they weren't alone, that countless other women have been where they are. There is power in hearing me too. It's very isolating to think that you are going through something alone. Knowing that others have been where you are just might be the thing that actually brings you out of it.

"That's why I am here today. I want women to know that they are not alone. I'm here to say *Me too.* I've been where you are, and I am here to help. I am here to bring light to the stigma, to push for change, to make things happen. I feel their pain and they are sooooo worthy!

"If you were to take a walk in my postpartum shoes, I would hope that you would be as tough as me, because most days even I didn't think I was gonna make it, but I did. And I'm not afraid to say it. Postpartum is my truth. An ugly truth that I just so happen to be on my way to conquering.

"It would be a lot easier for me, and other women struggling like me, if our government made mothers and their babies a priority.

"I cannot even put into words how terrifying it is when your mind betrays you.

"I'll leave you with this, though. I am a talker by nature and profession. I am an over-sharer by nature and profession. I got PPD, and it was the first time in my life I didn't want anybody to know any detail about what I was going through.

"We need to change the way we treat mental health. We need to erase the stigma and, if you don't mind, we need to take a moment of silence for the women I once thought should burn in hell, the ones who hurt themselves and their babies. The ones who didn't make it out of postpartum depression.

"Thank you."

Tears were streaming down my face and the faces of countless strangers who were listening to my speech. I did my part. I brought them into the Darkness. That was my goal, to make them understand, to make them feel, to make them care enough to push for change. The Darkness, it's so far and so close. I feel it hovering over me, ready to pounce. And, in my weakest moments, it does.

I was on Capitol Hill trying to protect mommas and their babies, but this momma right here, she's running a race against the Darkness, and the Darkness is catching up. This momma right here lost her forever and her job, and the Darkness knows this and is taunting her. This momma right here is wondering if she will ever not feel the effects of what PPD did to her. The Darkness, zero fucks given.

I have a love-hate relationship with the Darkness. It took so much from me, so much, but the Darkness also gave me a level of empathy I never even thought possible, and for that I am thankful, I am grateful. Empathy is everything, and I have that.

Dear World

DEAR WORLD,

I've given you a present, and I am begging you to handle it with care. It means the world to me and I am trusting you with it.

I am nervous. I don't know if you can handle such a precious gift, but I need you to understand the importance of doing it right.

She is innocent. She is learning every day, and she will soak up everything around her. What will you teach her?

Will you teach her love and acceptance? That you are her playground? That her opportunities are endless? Or will you show her a darker side? Will you teach her to hate? Will you suck the potential out of her?

You see, World, I have always been a firm believer that it takes a village to raise a child, but lately your village has led me to question that mentality.

World, I promise to do my part because I know that her becoming a good person begins on the home front, that it starts with me and her dad, but we can't do it all. She will spend just as much time with you as she does with us.

So basically, World, take care of my babies because, if you don't, I'm gonna have to kick your ass.

Mommy Unicorn

I'VE STARTED AND stopped this chapter multiple times. I want to find the right words, to paint a picture. I do not want to mess this up. Words don't fail me often, but how do I write my love? How do I eloquently tell the story of how two little girls brought out the best and worst in me? Munchie and Smoochie came into my world and shook it the hell up.

Through no fault of their own, their very existence is tied to the worst part of my life. After each of their births, I suffered immensely. Postpartum depression and anxiety grabbed hold of me, sucked the life out of me, and left me to die. Other mothers fondly remember the birth of their children. For me, it was the beginning of the end. My mental health was immediately compromised.

I used to think that marriage was the hardest thing that I'd ever do. I was wrong. My marriage was very difficult and hard as hell to navigate, but nothing and no one could have prepared me for motherhood.

Motherhood has allowed me to see the best and worst in myself. I have these moments when I am so proud of how I handled something, but then they are rapidly followed up with a loss of patience and then straight mommy guilt for losing said patience. Sometimes I am so overjoyed and I believe I have a good grasp on what I'm doing . . . and then—wham!—a curveball.

Once, it was costume day at Munchie's school. I didn't know that until Superman ran in front of my car and twin princesses waved hi to us. "Mom, I forgot my costume!" Tears, so many tears. I was heartbroken for her. "Everybody is gonna have a costume but me!" More tears.

"No, they're not. Get in the car. We can get you one."

She chose not to be late to school and instead went costumeless. I found a foam finger in my trunk and slid it on her hand. She was not really impressed, but she went with it. This kid's a rock star. I knelt down and told her, "I'm sorry," and I really was. She had a million costumes! She would have shined that day, but at the time Mommy was in the middle of a divorce and jobless and had laid to rest two family members and her puppy brother—all while trying to kill it on TV to build college funds for her daughters. None of that mattered in the moment, though, because I forgot a costume on costume day and my baby was real-deal sad, and nothing hurts worse than mommy heartbreak.

Being responsible for two little humans is often overwhelming. Most days, to be honest, I am winging it. The thing is, I'm okay with winging it. Socks rarely match, sometimes they eat things I promised that they never would, and they probably get a little too much TV time, but my kids are happy and healthy and have amazing manners. My little people are good people. They don't like to see other people sad. They know God and they show empathy. These are the things that matter to me most.

The girls think I am amazing. They look at me like I am a superhero. They call me Mommy Unicorn. They think I can fix anything, do anything, be anything. They have so much faith in me, and sometimes that scares the hell out of me. Why can't we see ourselves the way our children see us? Why can't we love ourselves the way our children love us? I know love. I've held it, fed it, birthed it. It is the only unconditional thing I've known, and the only two people on this planet who could have given that to me were my children.

It is difficult navigating society as a woman. Raising daughters magnifies this. I want to raise strong women. I want them to know, regardless of what the world throws at them, that they are important, that they matter. Little girls are constantly told how cute they are and how pretty they are. I don't think people understand that we are constantly teaching them how important their appearance is. The value that we place on appearance is disheartening. I know people probably think that I'm crazy, but if you call my girls cute, pretty, beautiful, etc., I will naturally interject to thank you but also let you know that, more importantly, they are smart and have good hearts.

I had to learn to cry in front of them. They have always seen me as their pillar of strength, and I am strong. I know my strength. I know what I have been through, what I have overcome, but I am also human. Sometimes I am sad. Sometimes the current state of the world makes me angry. Sometimes I need to have a good cry and feel all the feelings. I used to retreat to my room and make sure that they never saw me shed a tear. An unexpected moment changed all of that.

One time, the big one snuck up on me in a moment of sadness. I quickly tried to suck it up, but I was already too far gone. She was four at the time. The look on her face as she saw her pillar of strength reduced to a puddle of emotions was shocking. It wasn't disappointment or even confusion. Her little face was overcome with compassion and she walked over and held me. I let her. She wiped my tears and she told me it was gonna be okay. She told me not to cry and that we would get through this. How did her little four-year-old self understand the importance of letting a person feel not alone in such a moment? It was an incredible experience for me. I was so proud of her. Her crisis management was top notch. I took the time to explain to her that I was having a tough couple of days. She listened intently. I told her that it's okay to cry as long as you pick yourself up afterward. She smiled at me and gave me an awesome pep talk. From that day on, I stopped viewing my cries as a sign of weakness and instead saw the strength in my tears. She has been the greatest teacher of some amazing life lessons.

Having kids made me appreciate life on an entirely new level. Growing life, creating it, I guess it makes sense that that would happen. What I was not expecting was how hard death would hit me after having a baby. Uncle Billy was a huge part of my life. He was Mr. Inappropriate in Every Sense of the Word, and I loved him so much for it. His death was completely unexpected and shocking. Even I was not aware how strong the love I had for him was until I lost him just a few months after having my daughter.

One day I am sure she will be embarrassed by one of her many uncles. I will have to tell her that eventually she will learn to love them for their craziness, their ridiculousness, just as I learned to love Uncle Billy despite the fact that his butt crack was literally always showing.

After he died, I knew I was going to find something completely inappropriate in his phone, so I looked through it with pure caution.

I found a picture of a vagina. There is a huge lesson in this— one I cannot wait to share with my daughters, when they are old enough, of course. If it were anyone else, I would have been purely disgusted, but sometimes there are people who rock your conventional mentality of the world and you love them even more for doing so, vagina pictures and all.

The juxtaposition of life and death is magnified times a million when you create life. You are also far more aware of all things wrong with the world. Daily, I am scared for these perfect little creatures that I brought into this crazy world. I am far more invested in trying to make sure the world is better, since they have to live in it.

It's amazing, though; even when I am shocked by death, by social injustice, by how scary the current state of affairs seems, just one glance in their direction cures it all because, for that second, all is right with the world.

A Sick Baby

I HAD FILED for divorce, wasn't working, and wound up having to uproot my girls and move back across the country. Just when it felt like it couldn't get any worse, it did. I started to notice that my baby wasn't really getting bigger. She was petite, and she ate like a grown man. I wasn't the only one who noticed, either. Every day, people would tell me what a peanut she was. BFC, who works in a pediatric ICU, was also concerned. I became so obsessed with her size that I started researching all different types of possible factors for her lack of growth. At one point I asked her doctor if she had dwarfism. My kid was so small that I started to think she was a little person, so clearly I needed some real answers.

Out of nowhere, she started projectile vomiting randomly. She became a totally different kid. Her usual energetic self became lethargic, where even the slightest bit of movement tired her out. One day, I sat her on the couch to tie her shoe. She held her foot out as I tied it. Her sister yelled from the other room that she was going to watch her favorite movie. As one sat quietly on the couch and the other one watched her movie, I figured I would do the dishes. About forty minutes later, while I was still tidying up the kitchen, I realized that it had been forty minutes of quiet. I instantly knew something wasn't right. Either they both fell asleep, or something was definitely wrong. I checked the big one; she was still completely enthralled by her movie. I headed to the living room to check on the little one, and I stopped dead in my tracks. She was sitting in the same position that I'd left her in, foot still extended, staring straight ahead. I called her name, but she didn't look. I walked slowly toward her, still calling her name but still no response. I was panicking. I wondered if she was having a seizure. I screamed for her sister and I called 911. My baby was still staring at the wall. I touched her, and she slowly looked at me. She didn't look like herself, and I knew she needed help. She was rushed to the hospital, and that's when the tests started.

We spent weeks in and out of the hospital. Different teams of doctors. Some concerned about her stomach, some concerned about her brain. I told the story over and over about finding her on the couch. I pleaded with the doctors to please figure out what was wrong with my baby. We were exhausted. Her little body had had enough of the vomiting and diarrhea, and my emotional exhaustion was at an all-time high. The doctors were perplexed. They didn't really know what was going on with her, so they always made sure to stabilize her and then give us a plan to see outside specialists. Whenever we left the hospital, I knew it was just a matter of time until we headed back, and we always did.

Paradox—a situation that is made up of two opposite things and that seems impossible but is actually true or possible. My body, mind, and soul were on autopilot. Straight go go go. Surviving has always been my only option. It's why I always sit facing an exit, just in case. It's heart-wrenching to watch your child go through so much—absolutely heart-wrenching. It's also heart-filling to see people near and far offer help, prayer, and love. It's so beautiful to watch complete strangers care for your child as if she were their own, and so ugly to imagine the worst-case scenario because you can't calm your anxious mind. I had to call on people to care for the big one as I cuddled with the little one in her hospital bed. Hospitals can be isolating, but the people in my life took shifts to make sure I wasn't alone. My cousin Shanna pulled a Dr. House and tested my cat's poop to make sure the cat's sickness had nothing to do with the baby's sickness. Best Friend Claire was living across the country but sent food to make sure that I was eating. Natan, baby's god-dad, literally sat with me through every procedure she had to go through. My people showed up. I was so grateful to find some beauty in the situation.

I started living in my sweatshirt that said "Still Kickin" on the front. I really liked and appreciated the reminder, and hospitals are cold. One day, the nurses came in and told me I needed to go do something for myself. I decided to go see my therapist, Beth—because, look, if a bitch ever needed therapy, it was now. It was raining, so, of course, I was wearing my Still Kickin sweatshirt. A young black man, younger than me, was standing on the corner of Olson Memorial Highway, shivering his ass off and holding a sign. I was searching for money, and then I had an out-of-body experience. Hazards on, walking across highway, sweatshirt coming off. He was crying before I even handed it to him, and so was I. He put on the sweatshirt. Now it's his reminder. By this point the light had already changed, but not a single horn blew. We hugged and I went back through all the cars (and there were many). As I continued on my way to therapy, I cried and then I thanked the universe for my friend Nora and for her

Still Kickin mission and that the people waiting on me didn't honk. I needed that moment. That one precious moment in such a terrible situation. Nora has this way of unknowingly teaching me a lot about myself and others.

We wound up back in the hospital during Mary Clare's wedding week. I was so stressed out. One of my best friends in the entire world was experiencing her happiest moments and I couldn't be as present as I wanted to be. I remember a sweet nurse sitting on the edge of the bed and telling me I needed to go to the wedding. She told me that I had to get out and breathe. She reassured me that they had everything under control and that baby would be resting anyway. I was struggling hard with the idea of leaving my baby for a celebration. In the midst of my internal struggle, I had someone give me their unsolicited opinion on the predicament: "If I were you, I wouldn't even think twice about going to that wedding." That's the thing, though; they weren't me. I know the importance of showing up for people. During her wedding week, Mary Clare showed up to the hospital and brought us food. I really didn't think I would have ever forgiven myself if I didn't show up for her. As a feeler, it would have been something that haunted me. So Best Friend Claire showed up to the hospital with a dress and shoes, I changed in the hospital bathroom, and we walked right out the door. I told the nurses I would be back right after the ceremony. My anxiety was high, and I had no desire to party at a reception. I simply wanted to show up for my friend like she always had for me.

A little while later, I sat in my seat watching the most beautiful bride I had ever seen. Nora, who was officiating the ceremony, said something that really mattered. She asked Mary Clare and her husband, Jake, to look out at all of us sitting there. "Those are all your people," she said. I instantly knew I had made the right decision. If I weren't there, that statement wouldn't have been true. It wouldn't have been all of Mary Clare's people. Right on time, per usual Nora. After the ceremony I rushed back to the hospital, changed out of my dress, and went right back to cuddling my sick baby.

We went through this for months. We are currently still seeing specialists. Occasionally there's a new development, but that's usually followed by a setback and they seem to cancel each other out. Lucky for me, my baby has an unbreakable spirit. My baby is sick and it sucks, but through the experience I learned some valuable lessons. There really is nothing that will test your strength and faith more than watching your child suffer, and showing up matters. When you love people, when you value their presence in your life, show up for them—and not just in moments of sadness. Joyful moments deserve your presence too.

Dear Daughters

I HAVE THIS unhealthy relationship with death—some might call it an obsession—and, as a result, I've been writing my daughters letters since before they were born. I just always wanted them to know how I felt about them, what I valued, and my hopes and dreams for them in the event of my unfortunate demise. If I die, this mom wants her daughters to have a step-by-step guide on how to rule the world.

Dear Daughters,

You are smart, you are important, you matter. I want you to know that the world is yours. Take care of it. It may not always take care of you, or even make you feel like it's yours, but it is. There will be times when you question how to even survive in a world like this. Trust me, I've been there. You will survive, though. You will work through it, you will learn from it, and you will be better because of it.

I should tell you that you can be anything you want to be. I'm supposed to do that. Instead, I want to tell you that there will be people who will try to hold you back. There will be situations where you are immensely qualified and you will still have to prove yourself. There will be times when you will have to work harder than others. Do it. You deserve to be happy and you deserve to be successful, but you also deserve to know the truth. These things are not impossible to obtain, but your gender and your skin tone may make it a little more difficult.

In these difficult moments, please call on each other. No matter the paths you choose, no matter the distance between you, always remember that you share a common bond. You are the only two people in the world who have shared my body, my blood, and who have used the rhythm of my heartbeat as a lullaby. I would never want you to have to navigate this world alone. You will never have to. You will always have me. You will always have your dad, and you will always have each other.

Daughters, please be smart. The world is beautiful, but it is not always safe. Buddy system, ladies, always. It's important that you know that your body is your own and you are free to do with it what you want—but can momma bear give you some tips? Love doesn't always last, but STDs do. Remember that, and protect yourselves. If nude photos are still a thing when you're old enough to read this, please be smart enough to never put your face or any other identifying mark in an intimate photo. It's okay to own your sexuality. I encourage it. Nobody, not even me, gets to tell you what or who you can do with your body, but remember that the internet does not discriminate and it will gladly ruin your life, so don't be an easy target.

Laugh a lot, do random acts of kindness, and go see musicals. I've never met a person who walked out of a musical mad as hell. Fill your spirit with things that feel good! Try your best to not hold grudges, and find solace in knowing that karma and the universe always have a way of leveling the playing field. Protect your peace of mind. Nothing and no one matters more than your peace of mind. Guard it with your life.

Focus your energy on things that matter. If it doesn't serve you, it's not for you—write that one down. There will be moments in your life when you mess up. Own up to your mistakes. Don't make excuses, and don't qualify your actions. Say sorry and mean it. You will hurt people you love, and people you love will hurt you, but try to handle these hurts with care. The people that love you—and I mean really love you—don't disappear because you make a mistake or ten. They love you through your mistakes. It was important for me to share this with you because I need you to know that I'm not perfect. When you feel overwhelmed, lost, and disappointed in yourself and your choices, there will always be someone who loves you through it. You will always be good enough, and I hope you never feel like you are not!

Music can get you through anything, and if all else fails, listen to Prince and Bob Marley. They are good for the soul. Read! Read everything, and read as much as you can. Travel. Go as many places as you can, meet as many people as you can, and learn from the experiences. Cultivate lasting relationships, but don't hold tight to toxic people. Speak your mind. Correct people when they confuse your passion with aggression. Take care of your body, mind, and spirit.

Believe in something bigger than you. Embrace your spirituality, and talk to the universe. Ask the universe for what you want, speak it into existence, and believe that the universe will provide. There is power in positive thinking.

Choose your best friend wisely. You've known mine your entire lives. When I first met you both, you met my best friend just a few moments later. Understand that family isn't always connected by blood. You get to decide who you consider family.

Not everybody has the best intentions. Pay attention to the way you feel around people, and always trust your gut. Be humble. Learn your love language and the love languages of the people you care about, and then do your best to love them that way and require them to do the same.

Pray, meditate, and try not to worry. Think, think, and think some more, and then react. Do your best to not respond first out of emotion. Take some time to digest your feelings, and then respond. Love each other always, protect each other always, and never forget where you come from.

This world is not perfect. I know you see that, or at least you will. I know that you can't imagine how people could treat each other so terribly. I know you will feel disappointed in your world and in the people of the world. You will doubt, you will cry, and you will be furious. You will lose peace of mind. It hurts my heart just thinking about it, but, girls—never lose hope.

In those terrible moments that test your faith, please remember the good in people. Remember the random acts of kindness. Remember the people who stood up for the less fortunate. Remember those that died to protect another. Remember NOH8. Remember the people who were not afraid to speak up for what was right regardless of the cost.

And if none of that calms your heavy heart, remember me. Find solace in knowing that no matter how much darkness the world threw at mommy, she chose to stand in the light and never lost hope. Do I feel helpless sometimes? Absolutely, but mommy is never hopeless. How can I be hopeless when God gave me you?

The two of you are my greatest works of art. Because of you, I love harder, find meaning easier, and have a reason to work harder than I ever have. Loving you has allowed me to see beauty in things everywhere, to see myself differently, and to strengthen my relationship with God.

Mostly, I pray that you live your lives with integrity and on your terms. I can't wait until the day that someone tells you that you can't do something or be something. I hope in those moments you remember who your momma is and you do it anyway, because I would expect nothing less.

I'll love you until the day I die . . . and then I will love you from the sky.

Love,
Mom

The Blind Mom Chronicles

MY MOM IS legally blind. She's been legally blind my entire life. Growing up, people would often ask what it was like having a mom who was visually impaired. I didn't know how it was growing up without a blind mom, so to me it was the norm.

Looking back, I realize that there are things that stand out. When we crossed the street as kids, our mom would hold our hands tightly for our safety but also for her own. We learned very young, and quickly, to navigate for our mom because she needed our help as much as we needed hers. We counted stairs, told her when pavement was uneven, and never corrected the way she wrote her name. Due to her poor vision, Momma Kathy has always crossed the H in her name instead of the T. That one is a staple, though. I would be sad if she changed that.

I was reflecting on my childhood and realized that, while our situation is very normal to our family, it's fascinating to others. I am asked so often about my mom and her vision. Reflecting made me realize that there are far too many amazing stories about Momma Kathy and how she "sees" the world. I'm amazed by her daily. She singlehandedly raised her own children and a bunch of bonus babies and did it with very little vision. Despite the fact that the world has labeled her as handicapped, my mom has always considered herself "handicapable."

She attended blind college and learned to read braille and use a cane in case she ever went fully blind—which remains a possibility. It was at blind college that she met her boyfriend, James. James is fully blind, and even though the two of them can't see much, it has been absolutely amazing watching them navigate life and love together.

I grew up with a woman who was often told what she couldn't do, what she would never accomplish. I watched her repeatedly prove people wrong. I guess it's not really all that surprising that, when James said he wished he could ride a bike, her response was simple: "Well, why can't you?"

Imagine the sight—a blind man on a pink beach cruiser and a blind lady running along side him with a cane. It sounds like the start of an insensitive joke, but it's not. It's a real life love story, and it happened. There's an old saying, "Love is blind," and for my mom and James it's not just a saying. It's reality. They can't see a damn thing but each other and it's the most beautiful thing I've ever seen. I love their love.

Momma Kathy is a gem and should be shared. This cute little lady is full of life lessons and hilarity, and even though she can't see, she's a visionary.

My childhood did some damage to my spirit, and because of that I have often been critical of my mother. We are so much alike, and we often bump heads. I think the flaws I see in her I also see in myself, and as a result I place some sort of blame on her. I used to wonder how my mom could be so forgiving of my dad. I think sometimes I was more mad at her than I was at him. She was supposed to hate him, but she couldn't and she didn't. I blamed her for so many things, and I saw her as a victim instead of the warrior that she was.

When you focus on the negative, sometimes the positive begins to fade away. This parenting thing is tough work. Motherhood is easily one of the hardest things that I have ever done. There is nothing I question more than *Am I doing this right?* I literally think daily, *I am doing the best that I can*, but is that good enough? Yes, it is!

Mom, I know you did the best you could. I want you to know that I didn't forget that by my age you already had four kids and were doing it alone while legally blind and dealing with domestic abuse.

I want you to know that I didn't forget that at any given time you were working between one and three jobs.

I want you to know that you were so clever at covering up the struggle that it wasn't until I was an adult that I realized that our house-camping adventure was actually because our heat was turned off and you wanted to make sure we stayed warm and didn't worry. We didn't worry, because we had no idea. Your creativity shielded us from our struggle for years.

I haven't forgotten the old-school music that used to blast through the house or you singing to shoes, broomsticks, and whisks.

I haven't forgotten the numerous kids you took in and raised or that you helped raise my dad's daughters even after he was no longer living with us.

I haven't forgotten your au gratin potatoes, which could never measure up to my grandma's but were pretty damn close.

I haven't forgotten how you literally are a Christmas elf. How every year of my childhood you would sit us down and tell us that Christmas would be different that year, that sometimes even Santa struggled, but then somehow you always made it happen. The boys and I had inside jokes for years about "the talk." The talk kept us humble because we knew the struggle was real, but we also knew that you were a walking Christmas miracle, and it was always our favorite time of year with you.

I haven't forgotten the great lessons that you've taught me: if I'm gonna be my own biggest critic, I better also be my own biggest fan and, of course, to always stay sucka-free.

I haven't forgotten your delicious crepes, you dressing up for every holiday, or the eighteen-dollar bubbles you once sent me:

Me: Mom, I got your package!

Mom: Did you like it?

Me: Yes, of course. You couldn't see the eighteen-dollar price tag on the bubbles, could you?

Mom: Hell no. Who the hell pays eighteen dollars for some bubbles? A blind lady, that's who. Well, you better blow the hell outta those bubbles.

I haven't forgotten, Mom. I know sometimes it probably feels that way, and for that I am sorry. You did the best that you could, Momma, and it was good enough.

I didn't fully understand the sacrifices she made until I had my own children. I remember calling her, bawling my eyes out, and proclaiming, "I finally get it now. I know how much you love me." When I was in college, my mom went along with a lie for me. Every time my ex called, she told him I was in London. He had hurt me badly and I wanted to get over him. Avoidance was needed! He would call and I would hear her: "Nope, still not back from London." She knew that I was hurting and she would do anything to make that pain go away. I'm grown now—like, real-deal adulting is happening—and I have my own daughters. I now know the feeling of wanting to protect them at all costs.

I live motherhood and it's not for the faint of heart. Mother-hood has shown me some of the most beautiful moments of my life. When our family dog passed away, my mom was hurting badly—for herself, for her kids, and for her other fur baby, who instantly became an only child. Seeing her in pain was heartbreaking. She's a warrior with a heart of gold, and she radiates positive energy, so sadness does not look good on her. As we laid there with our puppy brother, telling him good-bye, I witnessed something amazing. Each one of us was in our pain alone. We were thinking of ourselves, our own pain. I watched my mom make eye contact with each of her kids. I saw her extend a hand to Nicholas, tell Sammy he wasn't alone, tell Andre to come closer, and lay her head against my leg. That's motherhood! She was drowning in her own pain but still threw out life jackets to her kids. We went from being alone in our grief to united. As we walked outside the pet hospital, we huddled like a group of football players getting ready to hear the play, and there was no doubt who the quarterback was.

Katie

IT WAS THE summer before college, and I had just gotten my roommate assignment. The college recommended talking to your roommate before school started. I was super nervous to call the person I would be spending the next year of my life with in a tiny college dorm room, but I mustered up the courage and dialed. Her name was Katie. She was at a bonfire with her high school friends, but she answered anyway. We traded information back and forth. She was a dancer, I did cheer, and we both wanted to be teachers, so we had some things in common. Considering we had never met, the conversation went really well. I got off the phone excited, and then I realized Katie didn't know I was black. Now, I didn't 100 percent know that Katie was white, but odds were that this girl from Cottage Grove going to college in a tiny town in Minnesota was white.

My grandma was down with the swirl when being down with the swirl was highly frowned upon. She was 100 percent Irish, living in Anoka, Minnesota, and she married my black grandfather. We are talking straight civil rights era. My mom was born on August 28, 1963, the exact day that Martin Luther King gave his "I Have a Dream" speech. I take pride that I come from a long line of women who call BS on what society tells them is acceptable. But still, in 2003, I was wondering how to break it to my roommate that I'm black.

Despite being biracial, my mom has passed for white her entire life. I've heard stories of people treating her differently once they found out who her father was. I remember my grandma telling me about a time when she took my mom to school. The teacher told my grandma that my mom was a star student and so well behaved, "Not like those black kids." My grandma humored the conversation. She asked the teacher if she had ever met Kathleen's dad. When the teacher said no, Ma told her she would have him drop her off to school the next day. Can you imagine the look on the teacher's face when little white Kathleen walked in with her black-ass daddy? Just the thought of it makes me laugh. The rest of the story isn't so funny, though. Once the teacher met my Pa, she started treating my mom just like "those black kids."

I needed to talk to my mom about Katie. This was a real dilemma. My mom is always doing something. She rarely sits still. She's an on-the-go, get-things-done lady. I can't remember exactly what she was doing when I approached her with my predicament, but I will never forget her reaction.

I told my mom that I had a great conversation with Katie. She seemed really nice and fun. I then expressed my fears. What if I showed up to this tiny little town in Minnesota and Katie was shocked at her black roommate? I was fully aware that, if she had linguistically profiled me, she wouldn't have assumed I was black.

"Mom, do you think I should tell Katie that I'm black?"

My mom stopped what she was doing instantly. "Danielle, did Katie tell you she was white?

"No, mom."

"Then why should you have to forewarn her of your blackness?"

Katie, to this day, is one of my favorite people. She didn't care at all that I was black. The only thing she didn't like about me was that I always left toothpaste in the sink.

It was one of my first real experiences with understanding privilege, though. Most people get to go to college and be excited, and if they are nervous, it's probably not because they fear their roommate might be racist. I wasn't afforded that luxury. College was eye-opening. It was a reminder that I walked through the world a little bit differently than people who didn't look like me.

A Letter to My Daughter's First Friend

DEAR JACOB,

When you were two years old, you chased my daughter Munchie around the playground, grabbed her hand, and unknowingly captured her heart. You were her first friend, and she loved you instantly.

Watching the two of you play together and seeing the way you were both adamant about protecting each other led to my decision to put her in the same school as you.

You're five now, and I want to say thank you. I've watched the two of you love in such a selfless way that it has taught me many lessons.

I've watched her cry over you being in the hospital. I've heard her pray for you every night. I have witnessed something beautiful.

Her love for you is unwavering, and what's even more amazing is your love for her in return.

I will never forget the day it was raining and I turned around and yelled at the two of you for goofing off. You were trailing behind Munchie with your coat over her head, and I just knew you were gonna get hurt. "She's cold and she didn't have a hood," you said. You didn't want her to be cold. Your little three-year-old mind and heart considered her comfort.

I'm not sure if you know this, Jacob, but you are her person, her best friend in the entire world. Some days she calls you her brother. Other days she swears she is gonna marry you, but it's always all love. The look on her face when I told her that, no, you would not be moving with us across the country, because of course she asked, shot pain through my heart.

Your family has become our family. Your nana is our nana. Your mom is my dear friend and your baby brother Ryan was Smoochie's first friend. It was heartbreaking.

I am so grateful for you, Jacob, and the love that you have shown my Munchie. The hugs and laughs and the fact that, when she went by Baby Girl for an entire year, you proudly introduced her as such.

A little Jewish boy and a little black girl met on a playground. It sounds like the start to an inappropriate joke—but it's not. It was the start of one of the most beautiful friendships I have ever witnessed.

Thank you, Jacob, for making my favorite girl your favorite girl too and for teaching me so many beautiful lessons.

I Am Not My Mother's Child

I LOVE MY mom, but I don't want to be her. I don't think that I've ever wanted to be her. There's no doubt that she is special but I can't imagine navigating the world the way that she has. I want no part of that.

Since I was a little girl, I have watched this beautiful and intelligent woman be controlled by men and self-sabotage. Domestic violence kept her isolated, and I imagine her lack of vision kept her self-conscious. I never understood how I could want more for her than she wanted for herself. Did she not see what she was worth? Capable of?

I feel like I have spent a great deal of my life parenting her. My mom was seventeen years old when she had her first child; she was a child herself, so maybe her maturity was frozen in time. I was twenty-six, was gainfully employed, owned a house, and was married when I had my first child, and it was still hard as hell. She was alone and a damn kid. I know it was tough. I know the circumstances weren't ideal, and still I believe that she could have been so much more.

I have watched her start and stop things over and over again. She's used to failure and knows how to deal with it, so she sabotages success. She's been considered for multiple life-changing experiences, and every time she has doubted herself right out of them. She excelled at blind college, where the teachers loved her and the students were drawn to her. When the college wanted to bring her on board as staff, she found every excuse possible not to take the opportunity. She did this over and over again. Opportunities would constantly present themselves, and she would be excited about them and then watch them pass right on by.

I've never met a person who had the potential to be phenomenal be so complacent with mediocrity. That is my mom. That is so many of our moms.

I once asked her to join me at therapy. It started off as my session, with slight interjections from her. I wound up sitting back and letting her just speak. She cried a lot, and she opened up about how she didn't always feel like she was a great mom and how she didn't tell me that she was proud of me enough. There was so much self-doubt. I remember sitting there thinking, *I have to break this cycle. I am not trying to feel this way, feel the way that she does, in twenty years.*

There's a part of me that blames myself. Maybe she wasn't able to fulfill her full potential because of us, her children, but having kids did the opposite for me. It lit a fire up under my ass. Determination, drive, the ability to continue on with very little sleep, inspiration—my kids were my recipe to success, not a hindrance to it.

I walked away from my marriage for many reasons, but one of the biggest was for my kids. I was not going to allow my daughters to witness a loveless marriage and to think that it's okay to show so much love to your children but not the woman who birthed them. They are too young now, but one day they will understand the strength that it took, the sacrifices that were made, and how it wasn't just for me.

I value follow-through immensely. I think I value it so much because of how much my mom's inconsistency impacted me. Our relationship consists of a lot of love—but as much as I love her, as much as I am inspired by her, I am equally disappointed, frustrated, and angry with her. As kids we are often shielded from the reality that we are living. I knew bits and pieces about our poverty and witnessed violence and horrible acts of disloyalty, but my child mind didn't allow me to really comprehend those experiences.

My adult mind, however, is blown. It replays the scenarios and outcomes. It fantasizes and creates alternative endings. It sees her as a superhero and a villain, the protagonist and antagonist of my life story.

I've spent so much time doubting myself. It's a learned behavior. I watched this beautiful lady pick herself apart for years. Like her, I searched for acceptance and reassurance. Maybe that's why it's so disheartening. To see her to continue to need others to validate her. I remember that. I remember wanting, needing people to love and accept me. And because you can't please everyone, I remember how awful it felt trying. Zero Fucks Given Island is so much better than Need for Approval Island. I want her here with me, and she deserves to be here with me . . . but she won't come. I visit her sometimes, but it hurts. I see a mirror image of the woman I used to be.

Because our relationship was never what I hoped for, I have always migrated toward strong, passionate, independent older women. I've made them my mentors, my friends, my family. I have built a tribe. It doesn't mean that I love my mom any less. I'm just aware that she's not capable of giving what I need.

When I started nannying for Jill May, I instantly knew that I wanted her to be one of those women. She was smart, funny, and compassionate, and she showed up for me all of the time. Pageants, hospital stays, my wedding—ever present. She was right on time. I needed someone like her. Her kids are now grown and I now have kids of my own, but her presence in my life was needed, wanted, and accepted with open arms.

I knew that Ms. Hanson, my senior year English teacher, loved me when she very bluntly asked me if I was pregnant. I had spent a week falling asleep in her class, and she was concerned. She called me into the hallway and asked. I wasn't pregnant. I was tired! But I loved that she kept it real with me, so I kept her in my life. It's been over a decade, and she is my friend. She has cried with me and laughed with me, and even though she's been married for years, she still lets me call her Ms. Hanson. Ms. Hanson showed up in a seventeen-year-old girl's life and changed it.

Momma Missy found me. She was partnering with the radio station I worked with at the time, and when she found out I was running for Miss Minnesota, she sponsored me. I was twenty-one, and I was drawn to her spirit. She was a hustler, a boss! She spoke her damn mind and she never really wavered in who she was. She was also a recovering alcoholic, and watching her choose daily to fight the good fight was inspiring. No one has taken me in like Momma Missy has. She takes care of me and the girls like we are hers. It's so beautiful to realize that family isn't always defined by blood. Momma Missy is my shero. I am motivated and inspired by her, and I want her to be proud of me. I strive to make her proud.

My mom cannot be replaced—I am fully aware of this—but

as a survivalist, it was always necessary for me to figure out my way. My mom wasn't good at teaching me about finding my way. I've learned more about losing my way from her. I think my mom lost her way. I'm not sure why or how, but it happened. I wish she could see herself the way that I see her. I see so much potential. I always have. I've learned so very much from her struggle . . . so very much. It would have just been nice to also learn from her triumph. There's still time, though. I think I'll invite her to Zero Fucks Given Island again, just in case she's changed her mind.

#BlackGirlMagic

I HAVEN'T ALWAYS embraced my black girl magic. Truthfully, I haven't always loved myself entirely. I do now. On every level, I love who I am. I love that I'm quirky and sometimes corny. I love that I'm emotional, that my intuition is always on point. I love that I am incapable of whispering and that my inside and outside voices are exactly the same. I love the mother I am, the sister, the friend that I am. I love my curly hair and I love that I am finally unapologetically black.

I don't know what it's like to always love the skin you're in. I was born into problematic skin. My brown skin has forced me into situations I didn't want to be in, ended friendships I believed would last forever, and been the catalyst for many sleepless nights. Racism sucks, but internal racism is torture.

I remember as a kid I would pretend I was invisible when black men were around me. I would hold my breath, squeeze my eyes shut, and will myself invisible. They scared me. I wasn't afraid of white men, and why would I be? I saw them rescue people on Rescue 911, save lives on ER, report on the news, and tell me the weather. The only times I ever saw black men were if they were wanted for committing a crime. Representation matters! It really does. Imagine never seeing people that look like you doing amazing things, becoming successful, or living positive lives. Without even meaning to, you start to view yourself and your people a certain way.

As I got older, my self-hate manifested itself in other ways. The amount of money and time I spent on trying to manage and tame my curly hair I can never get back. Fair skin, straight hair, that was the standard of beauty growing up. For obvious reasons, I could never live up to that standard. I knew there wasn't much I could do about my skin, but I tried hard to get my hair to act right. I literally used to have my brother iron my hair. I would lay down on the floor and he would iron it like it was a T-shirt or a pair of jeans. Now, at the time, I wasn't even aware of internal racism or self-hate, but that's exactly what it was. It's hard to love who you are when you live in a society that often sees your very existence as a threat. I spent some time thinking back through my Rolodex of pivotal moments that helped shape my identity, and let me tell you, it was disheartening as hell.

I've had people who "love me" ask me not to be so vocal about social justice because they felt like it was alienating.

You know what will make you feel real alienated? When a so-called friend asks you to tone it down on social media and stick to happy posts, like posts of the kids.

Or that one time in college when, although everyone knew you were dating, you were asked if you and your boyfriend were related because of course "all mulatto people are related, right?" And yes, that's the word that was used.

Can't forget the time black me showed up as Miss Minnesota and jaws dropped because, "Wait, you're Miss Minnesota?"

Alienation when you literally are not raising your voice, speaking steadily, passionately, and very intelligently, and someone tells you, "Wow, you're angry! Calm down, whoa!"

Speaking of intelligence: "Wow! You're so articulate."

I remember alienation as a kid. I went to an awesome-ass diverse high school, but I remember being at dinner with a white family whose kids also attended and hearing them make the most horrific generalizations and proclamations about black people—forgetting I was at the table, of course. I still feel some type of way about Olive Garden.

Middle school, when the cute white boy Jason was allowed to date me, but his sister would have been disowned if she dated a black man because, "You know, they beat their wives and stuff." College, when my sociology teacher said to an all-white classroom, minus me, "What do black people think, Danielle?" As if I could possibly speak for all black people.

Hearing a story about a robbery, murder, or rape and praying the assailant isn't black, not because you think they will be but because you're hoping it won't add to the ammunition against your people and because, for whatever reason, black people are always grouped together.

I've literally had people ask me why I don't talk black. I'm not sure how it's even possible to speak a color, but my guess is that the people asking that dumb-ass question think that I'm supposed to be ghetto and my intelligence confuses them. I've had people tell me that I'm pretty for a black girl. Um . . . yeah, that's not a compliment—like, at all. I've been followed so many times in stores that I've lost count. I won't even go into certain stores anymore because I'm not trying to feel like Julia Roberts in *Pretty Woman*. This is real life. This is my real black life.

"Oh, not black people like you."
"Can I touch your hair?"
"I'm not racist. I have black friends."

I really shouldn't have to say this—it should really go without saying—but you know what has made me feel the most alienated? Tamir, Eric, Oscar, Trayvon, Sandra, Jamar, Philando, and the never-ending list of lives reduced to hashtags. I have cried for more strangers than I can even count. Alienation is having to explain to intelligent people that all lives can't matter if black lives don't. Can you imagine screaming, "Hey, please see us, hear us, know that we exist," and literally having people do the exact opposite by screaming, "All lives matter"? I have spent countless hours and nights wondering why it is so difficult for some people to grasp such an easy concept. If you're screaming, "All lives matter," then Black Lives Matter shouldn't offend you—because all lives matter, right?

I'm so tired of people who complain that my reality disrupts their comfort. Must be nice to decide that you don't want to see and hear about social justice issues. How awesome is it to be able to turn it off? Unfortunately, I can't. I'm too scared of becoming the next hashtag. I've gone through my photos, thinking of the headline.

It couldn't possibly say, "Educated Mother of Two, Beloved Media Personality, and Philanthropist." That doesn't happen. I don't have a record, but I'm sure I have some sketchy risqué photos. Would they use those? See, those are the thoughts that have crossed my mind. Comfort is not a necessity, but feeling safe in this brown skin is, fighting for those who can't fight for themselves is, LGBT rights are, stopping the Dakota Access Pipeline is, making sure women keep the rights they only just got a few decades ago is. Making sure my Muslim brothers and sisters don't have to have a religious registry is. So, with all due respect, fuck your comfort.

In a world that doesn't always celebrate diversity, I've spent so much time trying to fit in and conform. I was a "good" black girl. I speak well, my skin is light, and I have dimples. People aren't really threatened by me, and that has come with some advantages. I benefit from light-skin privilege—not as beneficial as white privilege, but still I recognize that, just because of my complexion, I am able to navigate differently than my dark-skin brothers and sisters. I also know that it's not my fault. I didn't pick this pigment. I feel like people who are so quick to discredit the idea of white privilege feel like somehow it makes them bad or guilty. It doesn't. You can acknowledge the benefits of something all the while understanding that it wasn't by choice.

Sometimes it crosses my mind that maybe people have trouble with the idea because they don't want to question or try to dismantle something that benefits them.

I hold out hope that people are better than that, but I can't lie, I am literally astonished when people argue that white privilege doesn't exist. I have spent years trying to find the perfect way to explain it. I've failed numerous times. On a road trip from DC to Minneapolis, though, my big brother and I were discussing the current state of the world, and he did it, He came up with the perfect analogy:

White privilege—because no white person has ever been pulled over by the police and thought, *Damn, I wish I was black right now.*

I used to have this extremely vivid dream where I was being chased. I had it often. I had it so often that I started to realize it was a dream while I was having it. In the dream, I was walking and I noticed that someone was trailing behind me. As I started to pick up speed, so did they. I would pass a baseball field and a player would always be trying to steal second. When this happened I knew it was time to run faster, that they were catching up to me. Just when I was about to give up, when I was too tired to keep running, I would land at the doorstep of a glass house. What kind of cruel and unusual mind do I have that creates a glass house as a place of sanctuary, a place of safety? You can't hide from someone in a glass house! It was always my only option, though, so in the glass house I went. I would wander around looking for a place to hide, clearly an illogical concept, but as a survivalist, it's ingrained in me to make it out alive even in my dreams. I could sense danger, smell it, and feel it, and even though I knew it was a dream, it was still scary as hell. Knowing there was nowhere for me to go, I felt defeat wash over me. I backed myself into a wall, a glass wall, and I knew it was coming. I knew he was coming. He was already there, though. I slowly turned around, and I was face to face with my stalker. The only thing separating us was a thin wall of glass. His breath fogged it up and right as he lifted his hand to break it . . . I woke up.

I used to think the dream had to do with almost being kidnapped as a child. I started having the dream before the grocery store incident, and it continued for years. You know when I stopped having the dream entirely? Right around the time I started loving the skin I was in and embracing my melanin. So maybe that man chasing me wasn't even a man at all, and maybe my mind isn't as cruel as I thought, and the glass house is actually a symbol. Maybe for years I was running from myself, my beautiful black self, and maybe trying to hide from that was like trying to hide in a glass house—an illogical concept. And then it happened, just like in my dream when I looked through the fog and into the face of uncertainty and fear and woke up. In real life, I looked into the face of uncertainty and fear—which happened to be my own—I saw through the fog, and I woke the hell up! #StayWoke.

Stay Woke

"Racism's still alive, they just be concealing it."

—Kanye West

I ADMIT IT: I once lived in the sunken place. At the time I didn't know it was the sunken place because *Get Out* hadn't hit theaters yet, but when it did—hello, revelation. It's hard to get yourself out of the sunken place, especially because it's not really your fault that you're in there in the first place. My self-hate was taught to me, handed to me gift-wrapped from society. Here's the thing: it's much easier in the sunken place, because once you wake up, there's no going back.

Since I was a little girl, I have been involving myself in things that don't directly affect me. I would break up the fights of complete strangers, and tell people they were rude and "you don't talk to people like that" when they were disrespectful to a server or barista. As I got older, I marched for the rights of my LGBT brothers and sisters. I always thought, *Who the hell am I to tell someone how to live their life or who to love?*

I traveled to Sacred Stone to stand in solidarity with my native brother and sisters without question. I know that if a Muslim registry ever happened I would be at the front of the line to also stand with my Muslim brothers and sisters. I marched with complete strangers in Dallas for equality and was in awe of the marches around the rest of the world for A Day Without Women

This all sounds great, right? It isn't, though. It hurts. Because, even though I have been fighting for the rights of everyone for my entire life, I have encountered people who love me sitting in silence.

I have read their statuses complaining about the BLM protesters. I have seen their comments about Colin Kaepernick's "disrespect." I have watched them turn a blind eye to what's really happening to minorities in the world right now.

I have seen them constantly ask the wrong questions! Stop asking why protesters aren't at work. (Implying they don't have jobs is racist, by the way.)

Start asking why they feel it's so important to stand up for this . . . ask why! And then really try to understand the why. Dig deep.

Even more, I have had friends marry people with full-blown racist tendencies. Friends who I know love me, and still. I have been in situations where n-bombs were dropped while I was surrounded by people who loved me, and yet they stayed silent.

People who love me would stay silent when a racist man, who forgot I was there, dropped an n-bomb. Was his comfort and theirs more important than the horror I felt? The sadness I felt? I have had friends send me private messages to tell me that my black life matters. Thanks so much! You care so much about my black life that you privately messaged me! Awesome.

I have heard people tell me their disgust about the things they've heard people say, but did you tell them? Of course I share in the disgust, but did you tell them?

Do people care only about things that directly affect them? Do they not know how to be an ally? That's okay too, but I can promise you that silence is not the answer. The fight for equality is about human rights. It's about gender, about black people, and Hispanic people, and Native people, and gay people—all people—because all lives matter, right? Being selective in fighting for equality is no longer an option. It should have never been an option.

I often ask people what their "woke moment" was. Was there a certain moment in their life, a certain situation, that forever changed the way they navigated the world? I love hearing these stories. It's powerful and empowering to know what changed the course of someone's life. For me, it was a series of events that led to my wokeness.

I remember how I felt when Trayvon Martin died. I remember the questions that I had. I remember the anxiety that flared up thinking about my own child being raised in this world. I remember strapping her into a BabyBjörn and putting her in a mini hoodie and marching for Trayvon. I remember it all. Honestly, it's difficult to forget. Even if I was to find some peace in the situation, there was always another similar story ready to steal solace. There was *Fruitvale Station*, which chronicled the life and death of Oscar Grant. There were the videos of Walter Scott, Sandra Bland, and Eric Garner. There were Freddie Gray, Jamar Clark, and Tamir Rice. There were so many. Too many. One night, I reached out to Detroit and said that I couldn't take any more killings of unarmed black people. It was wearing on my soul, heart, and mind. I told him to be safe and reminded him that I loved him. It wasn't a long conversation. It didn't need to be.

I headed to bed right after that conversation. My heart

was heavy and I needed to sleep, but we live in a social-media world and I decided to take one final look. Just when I felt like it couldn't get any worse, I watched Philando Castile die in real time on Facebook Live. I watched a man comply and still die. Lives that turned to hashtags; those were my woke moments. So I came out of the sunken place and, let me tell you, it has not been easy.

I've been experiencing casual racism for as long as I can remember, but I had been experiencing it through the lens of the sunken place. I know that when I walk into certain stores I'll be followed. I've read many books and graduated from college and yet people are still blown away at how articulate I am. I know that when people tell me that I don't "sound black" they believe that black people are biologically ghetto and are confused why I don't sound that way. Black people, by the way, are not biologically ghetto. I was able to navigate casual racism because of a few reasons: I hadn't fully begun to love myself, society had made me a little bit internally racist, and it was easier to just deal with it as opposed to fight it head on. We had a black president, and I literally heard people claim that racism no longer existed. I felt the exact opposite. After Barack Obama was elected, I felt like I had never seen racism rear its ugly head the way it had after he was sworn in. I remember thinking, Man, it can't get any worse than this . . . and then 45 was elected and I realized I was so very wrong. Listen, be a Republican, a Democrat, be whatever the hell you want, but be a damn decent human being.

I'm honestly not sure what happened. I'm not sure if people think that the election of 45 gives them permission to be blatantly racist, but like I said, I was used to casual racism. This shit right here was next level. It was hard to comprehend and it challenged my mental health often.

There are so many examples I could give you, but there is one in particular that stands out. I had been working with a makeup company for about two years. I loved their work, and I adored the CEO. She did my makeup every Tuesday, and she became my friend. Every Tuesday, we had amazing conversations as she made my face fancy for TV. In the two years that we worked together, I never once felt uneasy, especially in regard to anything having to do with race. We did happen to disagree on Colin Kaepernick's silent protest, but many people did, and while I loved what CK was doing, I also could understand why she didn't. We were comfortable around each other, we shared secrets and dreams, and we confided in each other. I loved her and she loved me, so imagine my surprise when she dropped an n-bomb in my face. To be clear I'm talking hard r, not a.

On our very last TV Tuesday makeup session, she was explaining a situation that had happened to her teenage daughter and a guy. I was mortified at the situation. I didn't know the race of the man, and I didn't care. From what I was hearing, he was an awful human being regardless of what he looked like. I remember asking questions, none about race, and being very empathetic to the situation. She was telling the story and visibly upset, understandably so, and she turned around to grab a new makeup brush. When she turned back to face me, she put her hand on my arm and said, "Now, you know I don't use the word nigger, but . . ."

I didn't even let her finish the sentence. "But what?!" I interjected. She instantly knew I was upset. My mind was racing— *WTF just happened! Is this real life? She's only done half of my face, do I let her finish?* We were in the Radio One building. This was a FUBU company—for us, by us. *She just said nigger in Radio One. I'm hoping nobody heard her because I brought her in the building. She just said nigger, period.* She immediately began to backpedal. "You look mad. Are you upset? If he were white, I would have said that white motherfucker." Um, not the same, considering the hate, and historical context of the word nigger.

She asked me again if I was upset and, though upset was an understatement, somehow I calmly responded that I needed time to digest what had just happened but that it was mad inappropriate. Shockingly, I did sit through the rest of the makeup session and even hugged her before she left. Straight going through the motions. I went into my office and I literally sat silent. This wasn't casual racism. This was blatant. I hadn't heard someone say nigger since I was a kid, and she looked me in my face and said it. I texted BFC and told her to please call me. I was about to throw up and I needed my person to help me understand. Her damn mind was blown too, so she really wasn't much help. We sat on the phone in silence. Every few minutes she would whisper, "I'm sorry, I have no words." I'm not sure if I expected her to have some magical way to make me unfeel what I was feeling, but that's what she was so good at. Claire was incredible at taking life's shocking moments and spinning them into some amazing lessons. Not this time.

I contemplated only working with my makeup artist on a professional level. Telling the network I wanted to work with someone else and finding a new artist just seemed like a lot of work. It was evident we could no longer be friends, but was it possible to navigate myself differently around her and still let her do my makeup? I probably could have, but that would involve a return to the sunken place, and I was now officially too woke for that shit. I spent the rest of that day and all night thinking about what I should do. It was a sleepless night. This wasn't just about a person that could do makeup very well; this was about a person

I considered my friend. So, the next morning, I reached out.

Danni: [REDACTED], the last 24 hours have been tough. When you told me about [REDACTED], I was mortified for her and empathetic. Nobody should have an experience like that. But I am beyond frustrated and hurt as someone who believes you are my friend that your anger allowed you to attribute the horrible actions of a man to his race and skin color. You literally looked me in my face and said, "You know I don't use the word nigger, BUT . . ." But what? How does that sentence end? But he's a nigger? And how on earth did you think I would respond to that? Like, "Yes girl, this is the exception the rule . . . you should totally call him on that." I had trouble sleeping last night and even this morning I am like WTF. You can't be my friend, [know] how much I fight for social justice, and be able to say the word nigger to me. That's insane. That dude was a bad dude because he was a bad dude . . . it had NOTHING to do with his skin color. When you told me the story I literally was like what an awful human being. I didn't think wow he's awful because he's black, white, purple, etc. . . . he was just an evil person. To you, his evilness was equivalent to his blackness . . . I have been sick to my stomach and I needed you to know.

[REDACTED]: I am sorry you feel that way! Not sure I read this correctly, are you saying we are no longer friends? Danni, you have no idea what I've been through lately. Have you texted me to ask how I am? And you are entitled to your opinion. If they [were] any color I would have probably said something horrible. My husband's 2 best friends are black. I love them dearly. I will not make this a tit for tat, I have been there for you and true blue loyal. I will never bring up the stuff that has come out of your mouth when you have been angry. We all make mistakes. You touch my kid I may go off and say something that I didn't mean but I'm only human Danni.

What? What does any of this have to do with the conversation at hand?

Never tell a black person how many black friends you have. EVER!

Why is the focus friendship?

Danni: No this didn't say anything about us not being friends.

[REDACTED]: I certainly hope this stays between us about my child. Worst experience of my life.

I can imagine. But we're talking about racism, not your daughter now.

Danni: I am more offended by your response. WOW.

[REDACTED]: How? I thought that a call would be better. Texts are very unfair and can be misunderstood. Still not sure why you're offended. My SINCERE apologies for offending you. It was never my intention . . . I love and adore you. Above says you can't be my friend. If anyone knows me [they know I'm] I am a love[r] of all races. My team of artists are all races. I can only say I'm sorry for offending you.

Focus! Friendship isn't the point and again stop qualifying your statement because "you love all races"

Danni: You flipped the entire conversation about what you went through. Girl you said nigger to my face. And then said I will never bring up the stuff that has come out of my mouth. LIKE WTF. I have never said anything even remotely close to a racial slur. And everything I do say I would say to other people. I was coming to you as your friend to express my feelings and you flipped it. When I'm angry . . . I don't turn to racism. Also, I said YOU can't be [my] friend if you say that. Not that I am not your friend or can't be but that any friend of mine wouldn't say such a thing. To clarify: you can't call yourself my friend and think it's okay to say nigger to my face. Also, I have zero intention of telling about what happened to [REDACTED]. I am talking to you because of how it made me feel.

[REDACTED]: Again, I am truly sorry. Not sure what else you want me to say. I made a mistake, as we all have.

Tons! Agreed. But I need you to hear me! Not make excuses, etc.

Danni: I came to you to express my hurt and instead of hearing me, you jumped to YOU HAVE NO IDEA WHAT I'VE BEEN THROUGH. No, I don't, and I am sorry for whatever you have been through . . . but what does that have to do with the conversation right now?
I appreciate your apology. Also having black friends clearly doesn't matter since I am your friend and you still said nigger. Have a good day, [REDACTED].

[REDACTED]: That was not cool. I made a mistake and from the bottom of my heart I am sorry. I'm not happy with what I said. But I can't take it back, just learn and move on. So I still can't figure out the statement I can't call you [my] friend. I would like to think we are friends and my apology was accepted. Can you clarify that for me?

Friends don't say Nigger! Clear enough?

[Later] Just tried to call you. I would like to resolve this situation. Heard your radio comment and talking would have been best. Not texts. Working now. Let me know when you can chat. I have a few very fair things to say on my behalf. Thx!

Danni: What radio comment?

[REDACTED]: I'm free to chat if you are.

Danni: I'm not. Cutting commercials.

[REDACTED]: All good Danni. You call me when you can talk. I will no longer text. Friends call and resolve their issues. Not sure about your comment at 9:50? Maybe I'm reading into it since I listen to the show but the last 24 hours? The fence? Totally felt like that was a slammmmm dunk towards me. If I'm not upset enough.

Danni: You're upset? Jesus Christ. Friends don't say nigger stop!! Don't switch shit on me and play a victim. I'm appalled! WTF. No I will not be calling now. You don't get it and you won't. And it's cool, I've experienced this my whole life.

[REDACTED]: This is crazy to me. It's called a conversation that we should have. We are adults!

Danni: But the audacity to dismiss what happened and now you're all upset. Do you realize you looked me in my black face and said nigger?

[REDACTED]: I totally get it! I'm upset about it!! What's wrong with that?

Danni: Making it about you is what's wrong. I can't do this. I fucking vomited over this shit.

[REDACTED]: I'm only human to be upset about it. It's not about me for god's sake! I'm upset!

I think she may be starting to get it?

Danni: I will never speak bad about [REDACTED] or you ever. But I can't live my life like this anymore. This is fucking horrendous.

High road?

[REDACTED]: So sad that you can't just pick up the phone and talk. I fucking made a mistake. Would love to def say more but I will take the [high] road on this one. All of the best to you and your beautiful girls. Nice makeup today! XO and I meant that sincerely!
The last thing in my life I had to do was learn forgiveness. It's hard but I will continue to acknowledge my fuck ups and move on. Nor will I ever reveal our conversations or speak bad of you. Still remain loyal
. . .

I. Can't. Even.

What?

Danni: No it's not sad. It's called digesting something that happened to me. You take the high road because clearly you are insinuating that I'm not. I had an alcoholic abusive father. I learned forgiveness. I don't need a lesson on that. I do forgive you. What's frustrating is the conversation today. That made me feel worse than yesterday. I'm also at work.

[REDACTED]: Same! And you're clearly not the only one abused. My dad held a gun to my mom's head in front of me, Danni. There's a lot that none of us know about each other. I just may write a damn book too. Have a nice rest of your day. Again . . . my SINCERE APOLOGIES. Best!!!

Um . . .

Danni: Girl you just don't get it smh. All of your responses are so fucking terrible. I wasn't saying anything about my dad besides I learned forgiveness! Good god. Thanks for the apology but everything you are saying between your apologies is unbelievable.

[REDACTED]: You are wrong! I get it big time and I said something horrible that I wish I could take back! Done! Texting is so stupid! It gets completely misunderstood!

Danni: Yeah.
Just wanted to say you're right, you've been here for me, loyal, supportive, and I've appreciated it more than you imagine. But at the end of the day, if someone, anyone, in my life equates people's actions with the color of their skin, I can't put on a smile and feel okay about that. If someone is only okay with my race or loves my people as long as we act right, but as soon as they've done something wrong it's about race, then no, I am not okay with that. I accept your apology and understand you feel you said something you didn't mean. But I can't un-hear the connection you made.

Stop with the my friends are Black!

[REDACTED]: Will never come out of this mouth again. I am sorry and I made a mistake. Matter of fact I attended one of my bf's wedding this past Monday night. Gay and biracial!! I am NOT A RACIST and what I said sucked and was out of line and came from a bad place. Most of my bf's are black and you know that. I can't beat myself up over this any longer. I am sorry. Your friend, [REDACTED].
P.S. . . . you can always trust my word and I will cherish our laughs, tears, and long conversations.

Best!!

And on a funny note, most people think this little white girl has nothing but black in her.

SMH at ALL of this.

Jesus take the wheel

Note to All: Liking hip hop doesn't mean you have lived the black struggle

After her last text to me, I knew I was done completely. I felt worse after the follow-up conversation than I did when she said *nigger*. Coming out of the sunken place meant losing a lot of people. It's amazing how little we actually know about the people we spend our time with. To make things worse: After I decided to no longer work with my makeup artist and never said a bad thing to her, just told her that I couldn't work with her anymore, she started putting money back into the pockets of a company she knew was terrible. A company that she had spent numerous Tuesdays talking hella shit about with me. She even started doing the makeup of the girl who replaced me. Even worse, that girl has a brown baby and she has no idea the level of pettiness she was inadvertently involved in. Some days I want to crawl my ass right back into the sunken place, but I know confines of those depths could never lead to my liberation. And I'm not here for that.

#StandWithStandingRock

WHEN I DECIDED to go to Sacred Stone, I knew I wanted to help. All I knew was that there were some major human rights violations going on and I wanted to be an ally. I wanted to be supportive in whatever way I could and volunteer my time and body for whatever they saw fit to have me do.

It took us seven hours to get to the camp. I wasn't really sure what to expect, and I had no idea how life-changing of an experience it would be. After the things I witnessed and the people I met, how could I go back to my life the same?

A dear friend of mine connected me with the Six Nations. We were able to spend our time with the Haudenosaunee camp. It's hard to even find the words to describe the experience, but I will try.

My first thought when we arrived was that I was surrounded by good people, all good people, and that doesn't happen often. Here I was, looking at faces from many different cultures and backgrounds, from all over, with one common goal—to help.

It's not easy to put yourself in danger, walk away from your everyday life, and brave the elements and the unknown, but everyone there did. I met people who were just passing by and stopped to show their support, people who had been there since Day One, and people who would be there for the unforeseeable future. Hurt and humbled—that's how I felt the entire time.

Writing these words, I am trying desperately to capture the magic of the experience, but I could never do it justice. I watched men from California build a school for children out of clay and hay. I complimented them, I thanked them, and they told me that they were honored. I sat and talked to a veteran as we washed dishes in two boiling pots of water. He had come from Chicago as a part of Veterans for Standing Rock, and he was incredible. I heard his story, he heard mine, and we connected over our want, our need, to help.

I assisted in the building of things, organized, and listened to stories. I breathed it all in and I fought back tears.

I sat in a circle, by a wood-burning stove, in a giant army tent surrounded by my new friends, and we talked about injustice. We talked about a need for organizing and I thought to myself, *This is beautiful. This is how change happens.*

I learned that there were over four hundred different nations on the reservation. A cry for help went out, and it was answered. Different nations came from all over the country. Those who couldn't come sent supplies, money, and support.

I have never, ever witnessed people organize the way indigenous people do. I thought of the common sayings "it takes a village" and "divide and conquer," and I started really reflecting.

Right now in America, we don't really stand a chance. We are so divided. The divided, united states—ironic, right? That's how it happens though. Pit people against each other, make them hate, feel more powerful than another group or less adequate, and you can and will conquer.

After a long and emotional day of work, the universe did me a favor: it put me directly in the path of the emotional wellbeing counseling services teepee. I literally left my people and ran to find the entrance. I asked to enter, and it was there that I met

Madhusudan (a name for the god Krishna in Sanskrit).

He asked me to remove my shoes, and I sat across from him. The teepee was immensely calming, and I told him of my advocacy for mental health and that seeing this here meant everything to me. I asked him to pray with me. He took my hand and spoke all kinds of magic into the universe. He prayed for the water protectors, the children, the elders, the world, positive energy. I held his hand tight and I thanked the creator for the experience. I hugged him and, as I got ready to pull away, I realized that he wasn't, so I held on tighter and longer. I thought that he must have needed me as much as I needed him in that moment.

Water is life. Regardless of how you feel, there is so much beauty in people organizing and standing up for something they really believe in and doing it peacefully. People matter more than money. It seems like we've forgotten that. Divide and conquer is real. Remember that. I have native blood running through my veins, but that's not why I care. This is a human rights issue. I will continue to fight for women, POC, LGBT people, children, mental health awareness, and so on, because it's the right thing to do. Some of y'all really gotta stop only caring about the things that directly affect you.

Robert Frost

"Two roads diverged in a wood, and I—
I took the one less traveled by,
And that has made all the difference."
—Robert Frost

THE FIRST TIME I heard this quote, I was in the eighth grade and we were doing a lesson on Robert Frost and Walt Whitman. Though I love the poetry of Uncle Walt, this Robert Frost quote has stuck with me ever since. Throughout my life, it has been a constant theme.

I have encountered many people in my life who thought I could be doing more, should be doing more. I was told I was wasting my talents and abandoning my dreams. I have always wanted to help people. I changed my major a million times in college, but it was always about helping people—special education, social work, etc. My path took me somewhere different. Yes, my job is glamorous. I meet and interview celebrities, go to amazing shows, and laugh with my friends for hours during a live show . . . but for those people who think that's all I do: you are confused. I spend hours upon hours responding to emails from mothers who are losing their children to some horrific disease. They reach out to me because somehow I make them feel better. I help them laugh, and they know I will offer them support. I write to teenage girls who aren't sure they are making the right decisions, and I give them advice and love when I get emails back saying that they did the right thing. I spend hours talking to women who, like me, don't believe they can make it through postpartum depression. And the emails about marriage issues . . . don't even get me started on those.

Once I received an email from a concerned husband. He wished me a healthy pregnancy and then asked for me to reach out to his wife, who just miscarried, because she "loves me" and it would mean the world to them. What do I do with that? I do what I always do: I reach out, I cry, and I am humbled that in someone's worst time I bring them some sort of comfort. I am not wasting anything. I touch more lives than I could have ever imagined because I took this path. It was the only path I could have ever chosen that would have been right for me. Maybe I'm not even the one who chose it. Maybe it chose me.

Parts of my job are glamorous, but the best part has zero to do with the celebrities, the music, or the money. It's always been about the people, and it always will be. My heart hurt then and still hurts now for that couple, but I am thanking God for the gift he gave me, because it is a gift. Not everyone can do what I do, and now I am fully aware of that. I want to share one of my favorite emails that I ever received from a listener. It impacted my life.

"Thanks for the post tonight. I wanted to tell you this story of how you were my angel . . . Maybe you were an angel for someone else tonight with your post . . . I never listened (to your show) before April 2014. My kids (11 and 14) listened at summer camp and often tuned in on car rides. We went through a very bad divorce in between December 2012 and April 2014. My ex moved out at the end of January 2014 and my kids were just angry at the world and at me . . . The counselors said their father is/was emotionally abusive so they couldn't be mad at him . . . Lol! Long story . . . Bad roses episode (haha!). (Had I only known about roses before!) Everything was going south, my son attacked me one day, my daughter was mad at me for making her dad leave, etc. One Friday night after a particularly bad episode with my daughter, I prayed before I went to sleep. Not something I did regularly. I wished my mom was still alive so she could talk to my daughter and say things to her to help her see the craziness and the lying—that I divorced him after hanging on for too long . . . Things that if I said them myself would come across as defensive or bad mouthing her dad. That his screaming and yelling and hitting my son were too much. The next morning I got up early to take her and her friend to horseback riding lessons. Reruns of the show were on and he was talking about an article in *Vogue* about only 20% of married couples expect to be married for life. He said he and his wife would be married forever. They may be in therapy, but they'd be married. My daughter and her friend were happily chatting in the back but when I laughed for the first time in easily a year, they stopped talking and were listening. You then went on to say you loved Slim, but if you found out he was cheating on you, was not treating you or your kids well, or was fiscally irresponsible you'd get divorced. You said you watched what your mother went through and you would not demean yourself to live that way. I stopped breathing and almost burst out crying. In those two minutes I felt like my mom spoke through you. I pulled up to the barn and my daughter got out of the car and said good-bye to me and that she would call me when she needed me to come back to pick her up. She used a gentler tone and it was the nicest she had been to me in months. That day was a turning point to repairing our relationship. Things are so much better now, but that day was truly amazing. You have dispensed other sage advice and you all have made me laugh, which I hadn't really even noticed that I stopped before . . . Thank you for what you do, and I'm looking forward to you coming back. Be well!"

I love you, Robert Frost. It all makes sense now.

Fear

"Sometimes our dreams come true,
but sometimes our fears do too"

—*J. Cole*

WHEN ONE DOOR closes, it's not the end. Trust the process. It may not be your plan, but let's be real—sometimes we sell ourselves short. What if the plan is greater than you could have ever imagined for yourself? Hell, if I would have known certain things were on the horizon, instead of questioning or mourning a door closing I would have slammed the door shut my damn self. Trust the process. Do not live in fear.

Doubting often leads to greater faith, and it did for me. I've gone from grasping on to what seemed like my last little bit of faith in humanity to somehow seeing and feeling God working all around me. I do not know what's happening, but I feel it. I feel it in my thoughts, my heart, my soul. I see it in the way that I carry myself. I feel it in my interactions. I hear it in my words and in my voice. Mostly, I see it in my choices. I have made a conscious choice not to allow people to try to diminish my worth. And that is the key. Evolution of self. I found my self-worth, my #WomanMagic, and my #BlackGirlMagic, and it scares people. Hell, it scared me at first!

Fear is such a crippling emotion. Once I learned to let go of my fears, once I learned to face them, I started living a totally different life. When my kids were really little, they were fearless. Have you ever seen a kid on the playground attempt something that you know could end in his death? And even if you were to yell out a warning to him, he would attempt it anyway? Kids have no fear. It doesn't last forever, though. Soon enough, fear creeps in and they no longer want to take risks. Now the fear of the outcome far outweighs the excitement of the initial endeavor. Life is kind of like that. We are born fearless and quickly taught to fear everything, and then we spend a great deal of time trying to unlearn everything we've been taught.

Giving up unhealthy habits is a great thing, but you want to really change your life? Learn to give up fear. Fear of love, failure, acceptance, and success. Look fear in the face, channel your inner Beyoncé, and "tell 'em boy, bye!" You'll know you've conquered fear by the way people around you start to treat you. If people are constantly judging your lifestyle, commenting on the things that you're doing, wondering how you find the time to do things that you enjoy, and rolling their eyes at your success, you did it! I have never received more judgment in my life than when I gave up fear and was surrounded by people still living in it.

People say they want freedom but are complacent with living in fear. You can't live in fear and be free. It's just not possible. So cast your fear aside, and start living freely.

In My House

MY SWEET MUNCHIE once told me that it was Collection Day (Election Day) and that it was the day we picked the president, but that it couldn't be George Washington because he's dead.

My four-year-old, in all her innocence, listens intently, asks questions, and retains a lot of the information. I don't know a lot. But this I know:

In my house, I teach love, acceptance, and tolerance. In my house, it doesn't matter who you marry or what religion you are. In my house, we are critical thinkers. We don't ask why illegal immigrants are here; we wonder what travesty or horrendous condition they fled from.

In my house, I don't tell my daughters they can be anything they want. Instead, I tell them the truth. They have to work harder because they are girls and because their skin is brown. In my house, I tell them to treat everyone with respect and compassion.

In my house, I do not teach the golden rule. It's not important to treat people the way that *you* want to be treated; it's important to value how others want to be treated. You need to treat people the way that *they* want to be treated.

In my house, you will never hear "sticks and stones may break my bones but words may never hurt me" because words are powerful. So in my house, we choose our words wisely.

In my house, we thank God, the universe, and our ancestors daily.

In my house, there are two beautiful little girls who I have to fight for, and I will. I will fight with everything that I am.

In my house, my daughters will know that celebrities are not role models. They will know that their momma is a role model and their Auntie Bear is a role model. In my house, my girls will understand that only they have a right to their bodies. They may share their bodies with whomever they choose, but only on their terms.

In my house, my children will learn to stand up for social justice and do the right thing even if it inconveniences another person or makes someone uncomfortable.

In my house, we will not let hate win and we will not live in fear.

I don't care what y'all do, but this is what's going on in my house, and I would be honored if you joined me. Because in my house, the future looks bright, and I am clinging to that for dear life right now. Love and light.

PS: You are always welcome in my house!

Sticks and Stones

I'M SO GLAD I went to high school at a time when social media was pretty much nonexistent. How kids survive today, I'll never understand. People can be absolutely terrible. They can spew venom so easily when they are in the comfort of their own homes hiding behind a keyboard.

There's this amazing Dixie Chicks song—yes, I love them little country girls, don't judge me—called "Not Ready to Make Nice." There are lyrics in this song that speak to me!

> It's a sad sad story when a mother will teach her
> Daughter that she ought to hate a perfect stranger
> And how in the world can the words that I said
> Send somebody so over the edge
> That they'd write me a letter
> Sayin' that I better shut up and sing
> Or my life will be over

I feel this. I feel this so much! On every level. I have worked in media for over a decade. So much of my life played out over the air. Graduation, my first heartbreak, pregnancies, marriage, divorce—I have lived my life very publicly.

When the love of my life (at the time) broke up with me, started dating my lesbian friend, and then got her pregnant

. . . let's just say I was in no mood to celebrate Valentine's Day. Instead, we created a bonfire in front of the radio station and burned movie ticket stubs, prom photos, and all things related to that relationship. I think it was the first time I cried on the air. This was right around the time that Heath Ledger passed away, so, as we burned all of my relationship paraphernalia with Trina's "Single Again" blasting over the Minneapolis airwaves, we renamed my ex Heath—because, of course, he was dead to me now.

It was dramatic, it was funny, it was sad. It was real as hell. After that, something really amazing happened. I received tons of emails, and listeners kept calling in. They were shocked at the fact that I bared it all. That I showed raw emotion. I read letter after letter from women who related to my pain. They thanked me. The thing is, I was just being me. I didn't know any other way.

I eventually, finally, got over Heath. It was much easier to do knowing many people have been where I've been. I screamed from the rooftops that I was in love, that he didn't choose me, that he chose someone else, and it hurt! Through their letters, calls, and tweets, my beautiful Minneapolis people screamed back at me, "You are not alone. Me too!"

I said things people wanted to say but couldn't. I stood firm in my opinions, fought for social justice, and celebrated my #BlackGirlMagic and my unapologetic intersectional feminist mentality. I grew up on the radio. I put it all out there, and it was beautiful—until it wasn't.

Sharing so much of myself hasn't come without repercussions. I will never forget the day that I went back to work after having my second daughter. It was bittersweet. I was so excited to get back on the air but also sad that I was leaving the baby.

I was welcomed back to work with mostly open arms. I say *mostly* because, as the text messages flooded in from listeners who had missed me, one stood out.

UGH, WHY COULDN'T YOU HAVE DIED DURING CHILDBIRTH. NOBODY WANTS YOU BACK.

I sat there, in all of my postpartum emotions, fighting back tears. WTF is wrong with people? I get not vibing with someone's opinions. I understand not everyone would like me. I get it. What I will never understand is disliking someone so much that you like their Facebook page to tell them you think they are a terrible human being, bad mother, ghetto black bitch. Yup, that I will never understand. I will never understand being aware that a woman just gave life to a child and, rather than keep your hate to yourself, deciding to text into her job and tell her that it's a shame she survived. Are you seeing the Dixie Chicks connection now?

There are a million songs that will tell you how to get over BS. Taylor Swift told us to shake it off, and she was right, but that doesn't mean it's actually easy to do. I want to shake it off. I want to not feel like I've been gut-punched. I want to channel my inner Ludacris and think, *Move, bitch, get out the way,* but it's not that easy.

Sharing myself so publicly has paved the way to some amazing things. People who I have never met have impacted me greatly. I am so thankful for the strangers in my life. I have read letter after letter about the impact that I have made on the lives of others, and in some of my darkest times those letters have gotten me through. I am often astounded, however, by the pure hate that shows up in my inbox. I get a lot of love, but for reasons

I will never understand, all of the love takes a backseat to the few hateful messages that pop up. It's human nature. We ignore the compliments and dwell on the insults. What I have come to realize is that people want to be liked, loved, and heard. People want to feel like they matter. The truth is, we can't please everyone, but let's be honest—we spend a great deal of time trying to.

When I have openly talked about some of the nastiness that has come my way as a result of being a public figure—it never fails—I am always hit with the following responses:

—Well, it comes with the territory.
—You picked the job, so deal with it.
—Being a public personality makes you a target.

And so on and so forth. The thing is, yes, I chose this career, but how is that a reason to just accept or allow people to say horrible things to me? How does my profession give anyone permission to be hateful, vile, and disrespectful to me? Does me doing my job somehow make you feel like you have an invitation to be an asshole? Does me living my life impact you in any way? It shouldn't, and it doesn't. Sticks and stones may break your bones, but words . . . they do hurt, and they do matter, so think before you speak. It's really not that hard to be kind. It takes way more energy being an asshole. Trust me—I learned that during the ten days of filming *Bridezillas*.

Value Statement

I ONCE ATTENDED a workshop about personal branding. The woman leading the workshop was explaining that how we perceive ourselves doesn't always match the way that other people see us. She told us to list three things we believe about ourselves and three things that we believe other people would say about us. She asked people in the room if both of their lists matched. A lot of people's list were very different.

For my list, I wrote, "loyal, momma, and feeler." My other list said "loyal, compassionate, and good mom." My list wasn't identical, but it was clear that they were similar. The facilitator went on to discuss natural talent, skills, and passions. She posted a fill-in-the-blank statement:

I use my passion for _____,
    natural talents for _____,
    and _____ skills to make an impact on _____.

She then told us to fill in the missing words and that the final product would be our value statement.

My value statement read:

I use my passion for activism, natural talents for connecting, and communication skills to make an impact on social justice.

The point of the exercise was to help us understand that often how we view ourselves and how others view us may be very different. If we truly wanted to live authentic lives, our views of ourselves, the views of others, and our value statements needed to be cohesive. I wanted to cry. I sat there and thought, *Finally. This is me! Who I am, who I want to be. How others perceive me. There isn't a disconnect anymore.* I spent so much time in a space where my heart and mind were always on different pages and paths. It's so hard to feel one thing and think another or vice versa. Empathy, wokeness, and not holding back were an empowering combination. Postpartum depression, the deaths of unarmed black people at the hands of militarized police, and the decision to not ever be silenced again connected my heart and mind and allowed me to start living my value statement.

I think having a value statement can be very beneficial. It has for me. I feel like it holds me accountable. If this is what I value, if this is what I believe of myself, then I have to move accordingly. I can't say that I want social justice and that I care about women, black lives, and gay rights and sit back and do nothing when fundamental rights are challenged, when women still make less money than their male counterparts, and when I still have to explain that saying black lives matter doesn't mean *only* black lives matter but that black lives matter *also*. Living my value statement means I can't just hope for change. In order to walk in my truth, I have to be an agent for change.

I encourage you to sit back and think about the things that matter to you. How do you view yourself? How do you think others perceive you? What is your value statement? Think about it, create it, and then live it. Hold yourself accountable. There is a caveat: if how others see you is vastly different from how you view yourself, pay attention to this and ask the tough questions.

I had no idea that doing this exercise would give me so much insight. A while back, I thought about what I wanted and I wrote it down:

"I just want to have amazing conversations with people who want to change the world. I want to surround myself with people who are extremely motivated and passionate and who value social justice. I want to collaborate, I want to inspire, I want to not be terrified to love. I want to be the best mom I possibly can. I want to move on from past hurts. I want karma to work faster. I want to go hiking, travel and give hugs all the time . . . I want my anxious mind to take a break."

I didn't realize it at the time, but it was the foundation of my value statement.

Knowing who you want to be is the first step to becoming that person. I am so comfortable in my skin now. I know who I am. I have conversations with people who want to change the world. I surround myself with motivated, passionate, social-justice-driven people. I collaborate. I inspire. I'm not looking for love, but I'm not terrified of it either. I am the best mom that I can possibly be. I have let go of past hurts. Some took longer than others, but I did it. I have watched karma do some amazing things, and I hike, travel, and give hugs all the time. My mind is still anxious, but it does take breaks. This is who I wanted to be, and because I put the work in, this is who I am.

Pa

MY GRANDPA, WHO everyone lovingly called Pa, only told me he loved me once in my entire life. I remember it like it was yesterday. I was leaving his house after one of our many conversations where he would ramble and I would daydream. As I pushed the door open and stepped onto the first stair, I shouted over my shoulder, "I love you, Papa." I continued walking, not expecting a response, but then I heard, "And I love you too, Dolly." I stopped dead in my tracks. I literally stood in the driveway, confused by what I had just heard. Finally, a huge smile spread across my face and I continued to my car.

I've often been misled by words. I've ignored the actions of certain people because they told me amazing things. I clung to their words and excused the red flags that their actions were waving directly in front of my face. I did this in friendships, relationships, my career, and probably every other part of my life. I didn't realize it at the time, but in every interaction that I had with my Pa, he was teaching me an indispensable lesson. I knew he loved me, despite him only telling me once. I never questioned it. He was present. He was always present. Births, birthdays, first communions, graduations—ever present. He showed his love. In everything that he did, he showed his love. He was reliable. People don't really seem to be reliable that much anymore. I value follow-through. It is so important to me. If I say I am going to do something, I will do everything in my power to get it done. I don't like making promises I cannot keep. I would rather say no than say yes and not follow through. I never got the chance to tell him, but I learned this from my grandpa. He did what he said and he said what he meant, and I loved him for it.

At the end of his life, he was pretty much confined to a bed in a nursing home. I stopped by often to hug him and kiss his forehead. It was hard to see him clinging to life, struggling to breathe. Chronic obstructive pulmonary disease had gotten the best of him, making my vibrant grandfather pretty much a shell of the person he used to be. Conversations became harder to have, so we would often sit in silence. I would think back to the moments when he was so full of life, and I would try to etch the memory into my heart, soul, and mind. I was so terrified I would forget the way he smelled, the sound of his voice, and his laugh. He had an incredible laugh. One time, he was telling me how he had no idea how anybody watches the show *Friends*. "That Ross was sleeping with that Rachel and that Chandler is sleeping with that Monica, and don't get me started on that Joey. Everybody just sleeping with everybody. I don't know how you watch that show." I didn't have the heart to tell him that it was clear that he also watched that show, but it tickled the hell out of me.

On a trip home from college, he mentioned that his tank was low. He had driven an hour to pick me up, so I felt like an asshole. "I'm sorry, Papa. You want some gas money?" I was shocked by his reply: "No, Dolly. I'm talking about my life tank." I didn't have a response. I actually found it funny. Maybe he felt tired or maybe he was missing my grandma, who he had now lived without for over a decade. Either way, his life tank being low wasn't something I could even fathom. It didn't make sense. I was eighteen years old at the time. He was in his early seventies but looked and behaved like he was in his fifties. Nine years later, I was holding the hand of the greatest man that I have ever known. While I was holding him, he was holding on for life. His entire family was gathered by his side, and only when we all stepped out of the room for a second did he decide to take his final breath. I was so glad he misjudged his life tank.

My grandpa made me want to do better, and he didn't just tell me love; he showed me love. I recently discovered I have his smile. I don't know how I missed it all of these years. I knew I had my mom's smile. I just didn't realize the origin was Pa.

I think of him often, causing many nights when I wake up and he's heavy on my mind and heart. There are so many things I wish I would have told him, so much I wish he could have seen—mostly, my daughters growing up. I have so many amazing stories involving my Pa. I miss his voice and his calming spirit. I miss his flannels and sweaters. I never told anyone, except Claire because I knew she wouldn't think I was crazy, but after he passed away I couldn't sleep so I crawled out of bed in the middle of the night, grabbed my phone, and put it in my pocket. I didn't want to wake up Munchie, so I snuck downstairs. My phone started vibrating and freaking out in my pocket, and when I pulled it out, it said Pa was calling. Now, you know me, I was like, *Oh hell no.* We hadn't even laid him to rest yet.

My heart skipped a beat. I answered it, though, because what else was I to do? I heard nothing, but as I sat on the couch, I got this feeling from the very top of my head, down my entire body, and all the way to the tips of my toes. I had never felt anything like that before in my life! I just knew he was okay. I have never felt that feeling again, and I don't think I ever will. There is so much I want to tell the girls about the man that shaped so much of who I am. I will start with this: Showing people you love them is far more important than telling them. And those dimples we all have, we got them from him.

This I Know for Sure

WHEN I WAS fifteen years old, I fell in love. He was a junior, I was a freshman, and I couldn't get enough of him. About two years into our love affair, he decided to join the military. Before he headed off to basic training, he asked me to marry him. I was sixteen but I *knew* this was it, so I said yes. When he left, I listened to Brian McKnight's "From There to Here" on repeat. A little advice: in your moments of sadness and heartbreak, never listen to Brian McKnight. I cried for days, I lost weight, I wrote so many letters. None of that mattered in comparison to the time away, the distance between, and discovering that Brandon, one of my best friends, was my ultimate weakness. I had it all figured out, and just like that everything that I thought and believed no longer existed. The love that I had for him I was now giving to someone else. The future that I had once planned looked different than the one that I now envisioned, and yet it was all real in the moment.

My grandma died when I was thirteen, and I don't remember a lot about her anymore, but once, on a cross-country road trip, she told me something that has always stuck with me. She told me that, when she was sixteen, she thought she knew everything, but then at eighteen, when she knew so much more, she realized that she clearly didn't know much at sixteen. She went through this cycle of thinking she knew everything only for time, maturity, and age to make her realize that she never knew as much as she thought she did. I remember rolling my eyes because, of course, at the time I also thought I knew everything, but now it's one of my most valuable life lessons.

I don't know shit. I don't know jack. I don't know nann. It's safe to say that the only thing I really know is that I don't know anything. Just like my grandma, I had a tendency to believe that I had all the answers. You couldn't tell me nothing as a kid, teenager, young adult, or, hell, sometimes now. Miss Know-It-All, that was me, so it was a shock discovering that I didn't have all the answers. Once the shock wore off, however, I began to see it as a blessing.

What we know in any given moment may not always be true. It may only be true in that moment. I loved the hell out of the guy who went off to the military. I thought I was gonna be a Navy wife and stay-at-home mom. I really believed that, in the moment. I walked into my marriage and I knew that I would never let it go, that divorce wasn't an option, and that I would not raise my kids in separate households, but I'm writing these words happily divorced. The world doesn't give a shit about your plans or your truth. When I loved that sailor, I meant every part of it, and when I walked down that aisle, I walked into my forever. Life is a constant evolution of things—of thoughts, beliefs, love, and friendships. Life has a way of reminding me how little I know, and she is constantly throwing lessons of truth at me. It's my job to accept and recognize them.

Things I've said I would never do, I've done. People I thought I couldn't live without are no longer in my life. I feel like the last few years of my life have been nothing but a constant transition,

but that's life, ever-changing. Lately I've been yearning for sta-
bility, which doesn't make much sense. How can I yearn for sta-
bility but be fully aware that committing to anything scares the
hell out of me right now? I'm not even committed to the person I
am. I'm hoping that, a year from now, I will be a different, better
version of myself walking in my truth. Truth is fluid. Sometimes
it bends, sometimes it breaks, and sometimes it simply evolves.
My truth now doesn't mirror my truth back then, but that doesn't
make either any truer than the other. I've learned that multiple
truths can exist within one person, within one scenario, or between people. The only thing I know for sure is that we cannot
put all of our energy and hopes into a particular truth, outcome,
or story. The sooner we learn that life is a wild and unpredictable
ride, the sooner we will be able to navigate and grow through the
challenges and victories on our journey.

Empathy

IF I COULD give one gift to everyone, it would be empathy. The ability to feel, to understand, to connect to another person's misfortune or tragedy. Empathy goes a long way.

Our family cat was old. He was overweight, and he had been on his deathbed for a while. My mom, God bless her, is amazing, but she also holds on for dear life to our pets even when we all know that it's time to say good-bye. Puba wasn't moving anymore, he wasn't eating, and the only real sign of life was his shallow breathing.

I was on the floor, petting the cat, and I told my mom we had to go, seriously, this wasn't okay. He was suffering. My mom was bawling but finally agreed that it was time. My little brother Nicholas rushed home from work. Nicholas is not an emotive man. He prefers spending his time with animals over people. Watching my nineteen-year-old little brother down on his knees wailing was a heart-wrenching sight.

He was damn near hyperventilating, having a full-on heart-to-heart with our family cat. "Please don't go, Puba," he said. "I don't know life without you." He was right. Puba had been around for as long as Nicholas had. They really didn't know life without each other.

We got into the car and headed to the vet. I could tell you the details of what happened as our family packed into that tiny room, but all you really need to know is that we lost a beloved family member that day. We were emotional, all of us—even Nicholas.

As we headed out of the pet hospital, one family member less, tear-stained faces told the story of our loss. As we stood outside trying to gather ourselves, alone in our own pain, but also sad for each other, I heard an unfamiliar voice.

"I am so sorry for your loss." A homeless person sitting on the edge of the curb looked up into my face. I was overwhelmed with emotion. Pain registered on this person's face. It hurt them to see us hurting.

Here was someone at an extremely low point in their life, begging for spare change and with no place to call home, yet empathetic toward my family. It's extremely difficult to describe the beauty that I saw in that moment. It was life-changing.

I often think back to that day. It reminds me that the human spirit is incredible. We can be overcome with grief and loss, we can be homeless and in search of our next meal, and yet somehow, despite our own struggle, we can connect to another human being who is also in pain. This. Is. Empathy. If I could bottle it up, package it, and sell it, I would. Hell, I would give it away for free. There are far too many people that I have encountered who need a lesson or two in empathy.

If I pass nothing to my children except empathy, I will have succeeded. Empathy is hearing a story of a child falling into a gorilla enclosure or being eaten by an alligator and not instantly wanting to attack the parents. Empathy is realizing that the parents of those children have just experienced the unimaginable and judgment is not what they need right now. Empathy is not trolling people on the internet during their worst moments.

Now, when I feel the Darkness creeping up on me, I recognize it. It's not like before, when it blindsided me, when it sucker-punched me out of nowhere. It's gradual now, and unlike before, when the Darkness was always two steps ahead of me, I face the Darkness head-on and I fight my way out. I claw my way out. Losing myself again is not an option. Fuck you, Darkness.

In those times, I know I need to run. I need to be alone in my thoughts. I need to regroup and re-center myself. I am so thankful that I trust myself now. I know when I've had enough and when I need to put me first, call on my tribe, and protect my mental health. I need to remember London!

Once, I drove three hours to New Jersey and stayed alone in a tiny house tucked away on a lake. No running water, compost toilet, no Wi-Fi. It was heaven. When I walked into the tiny house, I was giddy. I was a kid on Christmas.

I'm kind of obsessed with treehouses, tiny houses, and Containerville. I envy people who can live on the bare necessities. I want to travel the world and only stay in treehouses and tiny houses. I felt like this place found me. Sure, I hopped on Airbnb and searched, but I'm smart enough to know that this place was given to me. A gift from the universe, right on time.

I fell asleep to the sound of crickets, and I woke up to the sound of the birds. My heart felt free and my mind finally clear. I had a day to myself and a great night of sleep, and on day two of my tiny house adventure, Best Friend Claire showed up. She drove up in her battered-ass Saturn and, like always when she shows up, I knew the Darkness didn't stand a chance.

We laid in a hammock, me writing my heart out and her talking to her insurance company about her battered-ass Saturn, and I knew I was gonna be okay. You gotta find yourself a person that instantly calms your spirit. Seriously, get yourself one of them. I look across at her, my person, my lifeline, and I say the only thing that makes sense: "I'm so proud of your eyebrows. They've come a long way." A perfectly ridiculous statement, so perfectly me.

Correction: if I pass nothing on to my children except empathy and good eyebrows, I will have succeeded. Eyebrows and empathy are everything. Beware of people who lack empathy, and never let a person with bad eyebrows tell you anything about *anything*.